MICHAEL COLLINS
AND THE
WOMEN WHO SPIED FOR IRELAND

We do not want in Ireland the absence of history, we do want a larger study of its truth.'

Alice Stopford Green,

Westminster Gazette, 11 March 1904

MICHAEL COLLINS
AND THE
WOMEN WHO SPIED FOR IRELAND

MEDA RYAN

MERCIER PRESS
WHAT YOU NEED TO READ

MERCIER PRESS
Douglas Village, Cork
www.mercierpress.ie

Trade enquiries to CMD Distribution
55A Spruce Avenue
Stillorgan Industrial Park
Blackrock County Dublin

First published in 1996 as *Michael Collins and the Women in his Life*
New edition published in 2006

© Meda Ryan, 1996

ISBN 1 85635 513 6

10 9 8 7 6 5 4 3 2 1

A CIP record for this title is available from the British Library

Mercier Press receives financial assistance from
the Arts Council/An Chomhairle Ealaíon

Printed and Bound by J. H. Haynes & Co. Ltd, Sparkford

CONTENTS

For Zelda and Gary

Acknowledgements

When I look at my notebook of names I realise with sadness that many people who helped to shape this book are no longer with us. But I am deeply grateful to them and to all the people who guided me from the surface to the depth of Michael Collins' work and especially his reliance on women to help him towards his goal of independence for Ireland.

The late Tom Barry was the first to tell me of Leslie's (his wife's) involvement with Michael Collins. This led me to interviews with Leslie Price, with Máire Comerford and Dave Neligan and I am most grateful for their assistance. I am also indebted to Madge Hales-Murphy who gave me some useful information some years ago, as did Todd Andrews and Emmet Dalton after much persuasion. Gratitude is also due to other contemporaries of Michael Collins: the late: Peg Barrett, Dell Barrett, Bill Stapleton, Vinny Byrne, Dan Bryan, Ernest Blythe, Seán Collins-Powell, Seán MacBride, Ned Barrett, Seán Hyde, Bill Hales, Siobhán Lankford, Mary Collins-Pierce and Kitty Collins O'Mahony. All these people gave me first-hand information and without them this book would be incomplete.

I am indebted to Michael Collins (nephew of Michael Collins) who gave me the diary found on Michael Collins' body, and Michael Collins-Powell who gave me other treasured documentation, as did Mary Clare O'Malley; to John Collins-Pierce, who trusted me with the *Memoirs* of Helena Collins and Mary Collins-Powell; to Liam Collins for his reminiscences; also to Liam O'Donoghue for the Nancy O'Brien letters. A further dimension was added to the book when Dorothy Heffernan and Máire Molloy willingly gave of their time and supplied letters and documentation in relation to their mothers – Dilly Dicker and Susan Killeen respectively. I also found original insights in the letters of Moya

Llewelyn Davies, given to me by Diarmuid Brennan.

I am extremely grateful to Iosold Ó Deirg who let me see Michael Collins' journals, which were written in Sligo jail in 1918 and given to her mother Sinéad Mason during a subsequent raid. I am also grateful to Maura Hales-Murphy and Eily Hales MacCarthy for access to their family letters in relation to Michael Collins.

A sincere word of gratitude to Domhnall MacGiolla Phoil, to his wife Mary, also to Eily Hales MacCarthy and her husband, Gus, who have been most generous with their time and advice.

I owe a special word of gratitude to Peter Barry, who generously allowed me access to the Kitty Kiernan collection of letters and gave permission to reproduce material from it.

I greatly appreciate the assistance and courtesy of the staff of the following bodies and thank them for access to and permission to quote from the archives in their care: Seamus Helferty, Kerry Holland and staff at the Archives Department of University College, Dublin; the Mulcahy Trust (the papers of Richard Mulcahy); Commandant Peter Young, Military Archivist and his staff; Gerry Lyne and staff at the National Library; Dr Bernard Meehan and staff of the manuscript department, Trinity College, Dublin; the Director and staff of the National Archives, the State Paper Office and Public Records Office; Niamh O'Sullivan, Archivist, and staff at Kilmainham Museum; Stella Cherry, Curator, Samantha Melia and other staff in the Cork Public Museum; the British Library Newspaper Board; Noel Crowley and staff at Ennis County Library; John Eustace and the library staff at Mary Immaculate College, University of Limerick; also Bríd Frawley at the University of Limerick.

I valued the positive response of the many people who gave interviews and helped me over my years of research: Dan Cahalane, Frank Aiken, Dr Ned Barrett, Jim Kearney, Bill Powell, John Toolan, Tom McCarthy, Tony Killeen, Josephine

Griffin, Mary Banotti, Andy Tierney, John L. O'Sullivan, Todd Andrews, Ernest Blythe, D. V. Horgan, Margaret Helen, Criostóir de Baróid, Seán MacBride, Dave Neligan.

I realised that finding photographs of those who lived in the early part of this century would be difficult. Therefore I am most grateful to those who went out of their way to contact other family members and did not spare themselves in locating photos: Michael Collins, Iosold Ó Deirg, Dorothy Heffernan, Máire Molloy, Ned O'Sullivan, Michael Collins-Powell, Helen Litton, Eily Hales-MacCarthy, Maura Murphy, Sylvester Barrett, Declan Heffernan, Ann Barrett, Josie Barrett-Leahy.

A sincere thank you is due to Jo O'Donoghue, editor of Marino Books/Mercier Press, who worked with me unstintingly through the final drafts of the manuscript, and also to Anne O'Donnell and Siobhán Cullen.

Thanks is also due to the many who could not help directly but who took the trouble to write or telephone me with snippets of information. A special word of gratitude is due to the members of my family and to my many relatives and friends for their patience throughout my years of research and writing.

The assistance of all has been gratefully appreciated and I regret if I have inadvertently omitted to mention any name.

PREFACE

Some years ago I began research for a biography of Michael Collins but almost at the outset I found myself drawn into the controversial aspects of how he met his death in an ambush at Béal na mBláth on 22 August 1922. Having grown up in west Cork, I was acutely aware of how families were split by the Civil War and also of the silence that surrounded the ambush. Men who had participated in the ambush agreed to tell me the facts of the episode, and as time progressed I found that the details of the final events in Michael Collins' life required a book to themselves. *The Day Michael Collins Was Shot* was published in 1989. When I returned to my research on Michael Collins I noticed that the role women had played in his life had, to a large extent, been overlooked. Coming from a family in which women were in the majority and where his mother Marianne was in charge after the death of his father, he got used to the idea of strong, resourceful women early. The adored youngest son of the household, he found it natural that women should love and admire him. He in turn appreciated and admired them. It was obvious to me that were it not for all the women who helped to shield him he would have found it impossible to evade arrest between 1919 and 1921. Furthermore he needed women as well as men to send dispatches up and down the country, women to carry arms and others such as Madge Hales, who travelled on a few occasions to her brother Dónal in Italy to arrange for a shipment of arms to Ireland.

Women played an important part in Collins' espionage. They never let him down despite being harassed on occasions. Collins depended on women, who had, in general, an easier time than men in evading the suspicions of the British authorities. When their cover failed and women like Moya Llewelyn Davies and Eileen McGrane were jailed, this upset the chivalrous Collins greatly, as the letters I quote in this book will testify.

I was fortunate to have had extensive interviews, on the basis of trust, with Madge Hales-Murphy, Máire Comerford, Leslie Price (de Barra), Peg Barrett, Emmet Dalton, Todd Andrews, David Neligan and a number of other participants in events with Michael Collins. They made clear to me how society women like Moya Llewelyn Davies and Lady Hazel Lavery were an essential part of Collins' intelligence network. I realised that the letters from Lady Lavery in the Kitty Kiernan collection now owned by Peter Barry were more complex than a first reading would suggest. The records, letters and reminiscences of Susan Killeen and Dilly Dicker given to me by their daughters, Moya Llewelyn Davies' letters given to me by Diarmuid Brennan and the memoirs of Michael Collins' sisters, Mary and Helena, helped me to understand this unexplored aspect of Michael Collins' life.

It was a bonus to be given access, through Íosold Ó Deirg (daughter of Sinéad Mason, who was Collins' personal secretary), to Michael Collins' journal which he wrote while in Sligo jail in April 1918 and which has not been included in any other book about him.

The Kitty Kiernan letters reveal much of the emotion, the turmoil and the great strain on Michael Collins' personal life from 1919 until his death in August 1922. These are important in portraying a further aspect of the man: his capacity for true romantic tenderness and concern. It is interesting to note that Kitty Kiernan is the one woman in his life who did not play any significant part in his work.

In interviews with Collins' contemporaries, I was struck by the fact that they all affectionately called him Mick, regardless of which side they had taken in the Civil War. This is the name I have chosen to use for most of this book.

Meda Ryan, 1996

From Woodfield to London

Michael Collins was born on 16 October 1890 in the family's stone farmhouse at Woodfield outside Clonakilty.

He was the eighth child and third son of Michael (Mike) John Collins and Mary Anne (Marianne) O'Brien. According to the memoirs of two of the Collins sisters, Mary and Helena, the night prior to the birth Marianne, always energetic and resourceful, had milked the cows and strained the fresh milk. The baby, christened Michael Patrick a few days later, in Rosscarbery Church, had a father who was seventy-five years old, but 'age did not make him old'. His father had married in 1875 when Marianne was only twenty-three and he a few months short of his sixtieth birthday.

Despite the big difference in age, their children remembered the marriage as a happy one. Since her early teens Marianne O'Brien had been used to responsibility and hard work and in this respect was to become an important role model for her cherished youngest son. She had to assist in the rearing of her many brothers and sisters because her father was killed and her mother injured when their horse shied as they returned from a funeral. And when she married Michael John Collins and came to Woodfield she had to care for his three brothers during her early years there. Her eight children were born in close succession, but she accepted her responsibilities as 'God's will'.

Michael, being the youngest of eight children, had a special place in family life. Although he was into mischief and adventure from an early age, his sister, Mary notes:

> To say that we loved this baby would be an understatement – we simply adored him. Old Uncle Paddy said as soon as he saw him, 'Be careful of this child for he will be a great and mighty man when we are all forgotten.'[1]

During the long winter evenings Michael would listen as neighbours gathered to tell stories around the turf fire of the Woodfield kitchen. The women, who often included his mother's mother, Granny O'Brien, would sew, knit or crochet. Embedded in Granny O'Brien's memory was an incident from the potato famine of 1848. While returning from Clonakilty she saw people on the roadside who had starved to death. They had been too weak to reach the Clonakilty workhouse.

Michael's father would recall hardships in his household during that period, when his own mother often did not have enough food for even a meagre meal to her family. Though the economy had improved by the 1890s, shortages still prevailed and conditions were 'primitive' at Woodfield. Despite disadvantages the Collinses were happy, according to Michael's sister, Helena. The farm was self-supporting. Grain grown on their farm was ground, made into flour and used by Mama for baking. Therefore, even young Michael's contribution was accepted with praise when he helped his sisters to pick blackberries for jam, took a turn at churning the cream into butter or lent his mother a hand at spinning the wool from their own sheep.

Papa 'idolised' his youngest son and namesake, and Michael became his regular companion when he worked in the fields. The five-year-old would listen to Papa's recollection of an evening in 1850 when Uncle Paddy and Uncle Tom discovered two landlord's agents on horseback who were trespassing and destroying the crops on the Collins' paid-up rented farm. The encounter which ensued resulted in the men being jailed for a year. This type of occurrence and other agrarian injustices soon influenced Papa and his brothers to join the secret ranks of the Irish Republican (Fenian) Brotherhood – an organisation which was dedicated to physical force to secure the independence of Ireland.

Michael, like the other members of his family, went to

Lissavaird National School. Under the influence of the head-master, Denis Lyons, this 'avid pupil' absorbed the history of the island of Ireland and the portrayal of 'patriotism' which was 'in the forefront of his teaching'.[2]

Michael was just six when Papa got very ill. A heavy burden of work fell on all members of the family so one Saturday in December Mama sent Michael to Clonakilty with the £4/6/8 weekly rent to the landlord's agent. On his way to the agent's house he saw a football, marked one shilling, in a shop window. He hoped that the agent would give him the shilling discount – something that was occasionally done for prompt payment. The agent's response was abrupt: 'Tell your father he's a fool to trust such a small lad with so much money.' The imprint of this episode lasted; Michael would recall it on his last visit home on the last day of his life.[3]

Young Michael had reason to remember the agent's rebuff because Papa never again took him to the fields. On a cold December night in 1896 Mama called her eldest son Seán (Johnny) to go for the priest. Papa had got a heart attack. The priest came and administered the Last Sacraments. As the days passed Papa's health improved but he would never again venture outdoors. Then on the night of 7 March, 1897, Helena said, 'Mama called us all at about 10 pm'. Mike-John, his favourite nephew, and the household's occupants gathered round Papa's bed. Though he knew he was dying, he had a message for family members and was lucid. Helena remembers: 'He was quite conscious when he spoke'.

He bade goodbye to young Michael, told Mama to 'Mind that child, he'll be a great man yet, and will do great things for Ireland'. Then shortly after midnight 'darling old Papa died'.[4]

Michael was reared in a district influenced by patriotic zeal. Jeremiah O'Donovan Rossa, the famous Fenian leader, had been born in nearby Rosscarbery and had once paid a cherished visit to his school. After his introduction to the

Fenian movement by his father and grandmother, Michael was further tutored by teacher Denis Lyons and the local blacksmith, James Santry. When Michael was twelve his teacher found him:

> Exceptionally intelligent in observation and at figures. A certain restlessness in temperament. Character: Good. Able and willing to adjust himself to all circumstances. A good reader. Displays more than a normal interest in things appertaining to the welfare of his country. A youthful, but nevertheless striking, interest in politics. Coupled with the above is a determination to become an engineer. A good sportsman, though often temperamental.[5]

As well as the fiction of the day, such as Kickham, Michael read O'Donovan Rossa's *Prison Life* and other political writings, including those of Arthur Griffith, a founder of Sinn Féin.

The older members of the Collins family were moving away from home. Tears had already been shed when Patrick sailed from Ireland 'for ever' for America. For most of his early days Michael's home life was dominated by women who loved and nurtured him. He helped to lighten the burden of Mama's work on their ninety-acre Woodfield farm. When he had fed the calves and completed the farmyard chores he could often be found kicking football, playing hurley with the local lads or having a go at bowling. But most of all he loved to wrestle, and would challenge older lads. His strength and firm build often gained him an upper hand.

Mama managed to build a new four-bedroomed house to replace the old house which had become draughty with many broken slates. The house, one of the finest in the locality, was later burned to the ground by British forces as a reprisal for a local ambush. Books, sent from London by his sister Hannie, or given to him by his sister Margaret and also Mary, formed the main decoration of Michael's new bedroom at Christmas 1900.

Michael was very close to his sister Helena but they had to part when she left home to become a nun. On 22 August 1901 Mama and Margaret sat waiting in the pony trap while Helena gave her ten-year-old brother a warm hug. Though his mother was still relatively young, her health began to deteriorate, probably due, at least in part, to the strain of work and responsibility. But the education of Michael, her youngest, required some thought. She was determined that he should have secure employment. Though his bent was for engineering and mathematics, and he was developing an adventurous enterprising spirit, Mama prized the security of a civil service position. When Michael was thirteen and a half she booked him into the civil service class in Clonakilty under John Crowley and John Blewett.

Michael's eldest sister Margaret and her husband P. J. O'Driscoll ran the *West Cork People* newspaper in Clonakilty. They offered him a home from home during weekdays but weekends found him cycling back to Woodfield in search of the outdoor life of farming and sport.

With absolute dedication Michael applied himself to his studies; in his spare time he learned to typewrite and wrote reports of minor football matches and bowling contests for P. J.'s paper. He was fifteen-and-a-half when he sat and passed the British Post Office examination, which offered him a position and a new life in London. The morning he said goodbye to Mama he knew it was unlikely that he would ever see her again.

Early on the morning of 19 July 1906 at Woodfield, as the sun brightened the farmyard, the new dwelling house, the valley and river beneath, Michael hugged his tearful mother, who was quite ill – so ill, in fact, that she had already bought material to make her own shroud. Sitting in the pony trap with his elder brother Johnny, he also bid a long farewell to the west Cork countryside. With money scarce and travel difficult, he knew it would be a long time before he would return. At Clonakilty he parted with his brother and his link with home, went by train to Cork, by boat to London and took up a position as a temporary boy-clerk in West Kensington Post Office Savings Bank.

FRIENDSHIPS AND ORGANISATIONS

London was an awesome place for the young lad from Wood-field but Michael was fortunate that his sister Hannie had been working as a clerk for some years in West Kensington Post Office Savings Bank. Her quarters at 5 Netherwood Road, West Kensington were 'destined to be his home for nine of the most impressionable years of his life.'[1]

Michael made no secret of his longing for home during the early days in London or of his wish that he could fish in the river, throw a bowl along the west Cork roads or do little jobs for his mother. 'Loneliness can be of two sorts,' he said to a friend, 'the delighted loneliness of the traveller in the country; and the desperate loneliness of the stranger to a city'.[2] For many weeks he was miserable but his letters to his mother did not reveal this; rather they reflected his concern for her welfare and his desire that she would take care of herself.

With his aptitude for figures he easily mastered his job, and was a diligent, reliable worker. The routine of office methods and clerical work would be of immense benefit in later life. He had the ability to make friends easily and was soon 'at home' with many of the Irish boys and girls who worked in the Post Office. With a view to promotion within the civil service, Michael successfully pursued evening classes at King's College.

His mother's letters became fewer, her health worsened, and just six months after Michael had left home he got word of her death. He bitterly mourned her loss. Although lack of money, distance and the demands of work were great, he managed to come home for her funeral.

As time passed Michael grew more involved in activities in London. He became an active member of the Gaelic League and the GAA. As a member of the local Sinn Féin branch he continued to follow the writings of one of its founders, Arthur Griffith.

By 1909 he had grown to a height of five foot eleven inches, with a firm physique, strong will and a need to channel his restless energy. In November 1909, fellow west Cork man and GAA enthusiast Sam Maguire introduced him (Pat Belton swore him in) to the Irish Republican Brotherhood (IRB) – the secret oath-bound society which favoured physical force to achieve Irish independence. He formed enduring friendships with other members. In just over a year he became section master and by 1914 he was treasurer of the coordinating body for the IRB in London and the south of England. At around this time he went through an 'anti-clerical' stage, as mentioned by his sister Mary, but later in his life he was a devout practising Catholic.

By this time Michael was spending every spare moment reading; his wide-ranging excursions through history and literature, guided by his sister Hannie, substituted for any gaps in his formal education. The nearby Carnegie Library became one of his favourite haunts. In addition Hannie introduced him to her English friends so that he would become familiar with their way of life. Her influence on him was immense. Her love of drama, literature and poetry became his love also.[2] Teasingly he would greet his friend, Belfast-born journalist Robert Lynd, who at this time wrote for the *Daily News*, 'And how's the non-conformist today?'

He built up a strong rapport with Joe O'Reilly, a man destined to be his life-long friend, and also with his fellow west Cork man and cousin, Seán Hurley. Michael and Seán Hurley returned to west Cork for Michael's first holiday at home since leaving for London, and spent summer evenings lofting a bowl, or playing hurley 'in the field above the house' with neighbouring lads. Seán's sister, Kathy, had married

Michael's eldest brother, Johnny, who continued to work on the family farm at Woodfield, and Michael loved to play with their children. Mick renewed his friendship with Bob Hales of Knocknacurra, a world-champion runner, and through Bob he got to know the other Hales brothers – Seán, Tom, Dónal, Bill – and their sister Madge, who would later play a vital part in obtaining arms for the Irish cause.

In April 1910 Michael took up a clerical position with the stockbroking firm of Horne & Company in Moorgate. At the weekly céilí he enjoyed his dances with the girls and his banter with the lads; his athletic build, dark-brown hair and boyish grin attracted the girls who were all 'mad about him'. His cousin Nancy O'Brien, who worked in the Post Office, observed how he avoided getting involved with any one girl, preferring to win the friendship of several. Susan Killeen from County Clare and a Dublin girl named Dolly Brennan had also worked with him in the Post Office and they were sure of a dance from him. He had, however, a particular affection for Susan Killeen – a bright, intellectual girl who received her education with the aid of scholarships.

Robert Lynd introduced Michael to London's society people. He became a regular theatre-goer and soon rubbed shoulders with the famous and the rich. In late 1913 this brought him in contact with Crompton Llewelyn Davies and his wife Moya (O'Connor). Moya was the daughter of a former Nationalist MP, James O'Connor, who had been imprisoned for nine years because of his Fenian activities, and Crompton Llewelyn Davies was Lloyd George's solicitor at this time, and solicitor general to the British Post Office. Crompton, who Bertrand Russell described in his autobiography as being 'strikingly good looking with very fine blue eyes' took a great interest in Irish affairs and was involved with his sister Sarah in the campaign for the advancement of women's education and women's suffrage. Through his friendship with the Davies Collins was introduced in 1913 to the Belfast-born painter Sir John Lavery and his attractive wife, Lady Hazel. Soon he took a keen interest in painting, and in his spare time could be found in the company of the Laverys at Cromwell Place, often staying for dinner or enjoying conversation with a select company during Saturday afternoon tea which was served in the gallery.

Though Lady Hazel had been born in America, being of Irish ancestry she always felt an affiliation towards Ireland. Her ancestors were Martyns from Connemara who had settled, first in Boston and then in Chicago. She met John Lavery – a man over twenty years her senior – when he was giving a lecture tour in America. After their marriage and arrival in England, Sir John introduced Hazel to London society. An artist in her own right, she participated in a joint exhibition with Augustus John.[3]

Hazel became friendly with a distant cousin, Elizabeth, Countess of Fingall. The countess was involved with Sir Horace Plunkett in founding the cooperative movement in Ireland, and belonged to the circle which included the writers George Bernard Shaw and AE (George Russell); she was also a close friend of Edward Martyn (another relative) 'one of the first men of his class and time to become a nationalist' and a member of Sinn Féin.[4] Michael Collins was not the only Irishman to frequent this circle – Sam Maguire, Pádraig Ó Conaire and others who were conversant with literature and the arts often accompanied him.

Michael's rich west Cork accent and his love of story-telling pleased his hosts. Stories of his childhood enthralled Hazel Lavery, who was 'beautiful, intelligent and a wonderful hostess', and who 'mixed her guests with gallant audacity'.[5]

By 1914 Michael had changed jobs a few times. Now he worked with the Labour Exchange in Whitehall. He had become a skilled debater, with the ability to assimilate facts, and always liked to consign to paper a summary of details. The burning subject of discussion among Irish emigrants in early 1914 was the continuing failure of the British government to implement Home Rule. Already the Ulster Volunteer Company had been formed in Ulster in order to prevent its implementation, while in the south a separatist group had formed the Irish Volunteers.

Michael Collins enrolled in the London/Irish Volunteer Number 1 Company on 25 April 1914 and acquired a rifle, with which he practised diligently. Around this time he contemplated going to live with his brother Pat in Chicago but first decided to visit IRB member Tom Clarke in Dublin. He told Clarke that he would become an active member of Clan na Gael in America but Clarke advised him to remain in London, as within a year there would be 'something doing in Ireland'.[6]

August 1914 saw the outbreak of the Great War, and the threat of conscription loomed for many citizens in England. Early in 1915 Michael, fearing conscription, took up a clerkship at the London branch of the Guarantee Trust Company of New York; if the worst occurred he could transfer to the parent company. He was reluctant to take up residence across the Atlantic and besides by now he had a regular girlfriend, Susan Killeen.

The Home Rule Bill, though passed into law, was suspended for the duration of the war, until such time as parliament would again examine the Ulster question.

In May 1915 Michael received information that the IRB were moving to take advantage of England's difficulty abroad. 'With all the impetuosity of twenty-five I went to Tom Clarke and told him I was ready to go home and do whatever he wanted me to do. But he was not ready for me to go.'[7]

During this visit to Dublin with Seán Hurley Michael took the train to Bandon and walked to Knocknacurra for a chat with members of the Hales family. Young Madge's eyes sparkled, according to Ned Barrett who watched her, as she hung the kettle to boil on the crane over the open hearth;

she threw a few blocks on the fire because she knew that Mick's arrival would mean a long night of debate. By the time day dawned all the company had determined that they would not fight for any country but Ireland.[8]

EASTER 1916

In late August 1915 Michael was summoned to Dublin. He and some of his friends were given a series of instructions, told to be ready for the call and to lay the foundations in the IRB London circle. For the rest of that year he was full of expectation and apprehension. Susan Killeen had lost her job in a London post office because she had refused to take the oath of allegiance and with Dolly Brennan and Nancy O'Brien she had returned to Dublin. But Susan was on holidays in Clare during his Dublin visit. He wrote to her: 'I don't remember ever being more disappointed in my life than I was on Saturday week.' He blamed himself for not responding promptly to her letters. 'But really I do hate letter-writing,' he wrote, 'and I'm not good at it and can't write down the things I want to say – however don't think that because I don't write I forget.' He was feeling 'lonely and despondent' and wondered would he feel better if he was back in Dublin. He poured out his unease about life in London, especially with the threat of conscription. 'I'll never be happy until I'm out of it and then mightn't either,' he wrote.[1]

On the night of 15 January 1916, the night prior to the introduction of the Conscription Act, Michael bade a sad farewell to Hannie, who had been his counsellor, helper and friend for almost ten years. With fifteen of his friends he left London and sailed for Dublin.

Through his IRB contacts he got his first job in Dublin. As 'financial adviser to Count Plunkett' he received £1 for a three-day week, plus lunch. During those early days of 1916, as he wrote to his sister Hannie, he was 'not feeling at all happy, lonely you know'.[2] However the adjustment didn't take long; at least he had Susan's support and love. Mick had a romantic relationship with Susan during the 1914–1917 period. They shared common interests in politics, history, literature and poetry. He had danced with her at the céilís in London and would transcribe poems for her to learn 'off'; she would recite them for him on their dates. They would discuss books, but above all they would discuss their shared interest in the Gaelic League and the future of Ireland.

Soon he got into the swing of Dublin life, meeting new friends like Rory O'Connor and some of his 'old associates'. Politically there was 'no reason for despondency,' he wrote to Hannie. 'In fact there is every excuse for satisfaction.'[3] He followed target practice with the Volunteers at Larkfield Manor, Kimmage, and before long got a new job in the office of accountants, Craig, Gardner and Company in Dame Street.

In January 1916 the military council of the IRB had set Easter as the time to 'declare the right of the people of Ireland to ownership of Ireland'.[4] Prior to Easter, Michael told Nancy O'Brien, Susan Killeen and Dolly Brennan – all three were staying together in Howth – that they should get out of town as things could get 'too hot'. But they were adamant that they would be on standby in case their services were needed.

On Easter Sunday a series of mishaps threw into disarray the initial plans for the Rising but by eight o'clock on Easter Monday morning 'definite orders from Thomas MacDonagh' to proceed with the arranged programme reached the Keating Branch of the Gaelic League, of which Collins was a member. Collins collected one of the organisers, Joseph Plunkett, from a private nursing home where he was recovering after an operation on his throat. He acted as his aide-de-camp throughout the Rising. During the week of the Rising, he had reason to admire the courage and steadfastness of Cumann na mBan members such as Winifred Carney, Elizabeth O'Farrell and Julia Grenan.

By Saturday surrender was inevitable. Pearse and some of the other leaders consulted together and in the hope of saving lives agreed to an unconditional surrender. With bodies strewn everywhere, with buildings blazing, it was an apocalyptic sight. Seán Hurley, Mick's friend and cousin who had come with him from London, was among the dead who lay at a barricade. The men who surrendered were herded into the green in front of the Rotunda Hospital, and surrounded by a ring of bayonets on the orders of Captain Lee Wilson. During the night many of them were mistreated and humiliated by Wilson. Michael was later penned off for deportation with a few hundred more of the insurgents. Over the following weeks sixteen of the leaders faced death before a firing squad. This in turn helped to sway public opinion in their favour.

On 1 May 1916, Michael found himself a guest of the British government in Stafford Detention Centre as Irish Prisoner 48F. He wrote his first prison letter on 16 May, to his sister Hannie, and told her of 'the heart-scalding eternal brooding on all sorts of things, thoughts of friends dead & living – especially those recently dead'.[5] Because all his life Michael had been so active, it is small wonder that time dragged – 'the horror of the way in which it refuses to pass,' he wrote to Hannie. He turned to books for solace and asked Hannie for 'a few good (& long) novels and for Heath's *Practical French Grammar*'.[6]

Towards the end of May he wrote a letter of thanks to his girlfriend Susan Killeen for her parcel containing 'many delightful articles ... It was very kind and thoughtful of you'. In typical fashion he did not want to worry Susan. 'Life here has not been so ghastly ... since we've been allowed reading matter and to write letters. Also we are allowed to smoke ...'

He asked Susan to get in touch with Cumann na mBan, to ask them to 'look up Mrs Kirwan of Maynooth whose husband is here [in Stafford]. They have five or six children who are not I am afraid being attended to at all. Also Mrs Little ... more or less similarly placed ... '[7]

Back in Ireland a big round-up was underway, with people

being hauled in from all areas. To accommodate all the prisoners, internment camps were set up. Michael Collins was moved to Frongoch, north Wales, a disused distillery. Before the move he wrote to Susan and expressed his unease, especially about letter-writing restrictions. Things had certainly changed since he expressed his dislike of letter-writing the previous year. He anticipated that letters might be reduced to one a week. 'Because,' he told her, 'you have no idea of the number of letters I've been writing ... some not fit to send anybody.'[8] Established in Hut 7, Upper Internment Camp, he was soon elected 'hut leader'. His high spirits, his cheerfulness, his daring, his leadership and organisational ability led to the name 'Michael' being affectionately replaced by 'Mick'. It was at this time in Frongoch that the nickname 'The Big Fellow' was first used about Michael.[9]

He wrote a great number of letters while he was in Frongoch and in turn received support from women such as Susan Killeen, his cousin Nancy and his sister Hannie. The *Independent*, which Dolly Brennan continued to send, kept him abreast of the news in Ireland. Most days he wrote letters. Several he sent 'surreptitiously' so that he was losing track of his correspondence 'which has gone all awry'. Parcels 'from home' were one of the great joys of prison life.[10] They were often sent by the women who, under Kathleen Clarke, had formed the Irish Volunteers' Dependants' Fund – an organisation set up for the dependants of Volunteer prisoners arrested and Volunteers killed.

In early September an attempt was made to force some of the London-Irish to join the British army. About sixty men would have been liable for conscription, having been domiciled in Britain since the outbreak of the Great War. When they resisted they were mistreated and confined to bread and water in a effort to break their spirit. The 'punishment' numbers increased, with the men 'being deprived of their letters, newspapers, smoking materials'.[11] Collins became chief organiser of a system which successfully got messages, food, newspapers and other items from the non-punishment to the punishment camp.[12] The satisfaction he derived from 'this game of smuggling and communication' made him 'happy' as he enjoyed outsmarting the authorities, and 'besides it gives some spice to the usual monotony,' he wrote to Seán Deasy.[13] Conspiracy and unorthodox methods gave him a foretaste of secrecy and manipulation, tactics which he was to exploit to the full in succeeding years.

During the winter there was plenty of mud and dirt in the valley after the heavy rains. Michael was awakened one night by 'a rat between the blankets'. He told Susan of this 'exciting experience' and his regret that he 'didn't catch the blighter either'.[14]

Frongoch was a splendid school. Mick would often conduct debates when the prisoners assembled at night. An inveterate scribbler, 'Mick was forever jotting down points in that notebook,' Ned Barrett recalls. That notebook he also used for names and addresses – important contacts which he was to utilise to advantage in later years.[15]

By December, detention of untried prisoners had become a problem for the establishment, so on Christmas Eve Mick Collins and some of his comrades were on the boat back to Dublin. Sadness lay ahead. When Mick reached Woodfield on Christmas night, he found the family and neighbours waking his maternal grandmother. Granny O'Brien had died during the previous night. His cousin recalled: 'He had loved this grandmother. He had not been home for his mother's waking all those years ago. I could see he was sad. Granny and his mother had the same features.'[16]

With himself having 'some kind of reaction' and 'poor old grandmother dead' and 'that brother of mine and his wife both very unwell' he would be glad 'to go back to Dublin' he wrote to 'Siobhán a Cushla' (Susan, my pulse). He was looking forward to meeting her, to being with her, after all this time.

29

Rather than by letter, personally, 'I want to thank you for all the kindness which you have been bestowed on me while in jail, *a Cushla*.'[17]

On his way back he made 'a few useful contacts' when he went to a céilí run by Cumann na mBan in the City Hall, Cork. 'He met the Duggan family and Nora M. O'Brien' who, according to his sister Mary, were extremely active later.[18]

Back in Dublin he had Susan, the friends nurtured in Frongoch and his other friends with separatist views. There was work to be done.

Women Aid IRB Reorganisation

Shortly after Michael Collins returned to Dublin he again began to attend the Keating Branch of the Gaelic League and discuss the future with the many released men. He became a member of the Supreme Council of the IRB. When Count Plunkett was put forward as the Sinn Féin candidate for North Roscommon, Collins canvassed during the January frost, snow and slush. The election was fought with the co-operation of members of Sinn Féin, the IRB, Irish Nation League, the Irish Volunteers and Cumann na mBan. The voters gave Count Plunkett a clear majority on 3 February 1917. Mick, in a happy mood, told Hannie he was 'pleased to see so many old lads coming out in the snow and voting for Plunkett with the greatest enthusiasm.'[1]

He now needed a source of revenue as well as a channel for his dynamic energy. An opportunity soon presented itself. Kathleen Clarke had founded the Irish Volunteers' Dependants' Fund (later amalgamated with the National Aid body) in the aftermath of the Rising to help to ease the financial burden visited on many families. She and other women had done Trojan work in this area by helping families in need. While the men were in jail these women kept the national movement alive: they were responsible for propaganda which helped to mould opinion to respect the martyrdom of the 1916 leaders; they had their prose and poetry published and they created a revolutionary fervour countrywide. Kathleen Clarke now needed a full-time secretary to coordinate and distribute funds collected through various activities, together with moneys received from Clan na Gael in America.

When Collins' name was put forward, Kathleen Clarke agreed: 'He was just the man I had been hoping for. He was IRB and Irish Volunteer and also reminded me in many ways of Seán MacDermott. He also agreed with my idea that the fight for freedom must be continued, the Rising to count as the first blow'.[2] Collins started work on 19 February 1917, at a wage of £2/10s a week. He was now in a position to pay for his lodgings at 44 Mountjoy Street, take Susan out and sometimes have a night with 'the boys'.

As a member of the Supreme Council of the IRB, Collins set about its reorganisation. He had also been elected to the Volunteer Provisional Executive, the body which was to direct recruitment. Throughout early 1917 there was a great countrywide recruitment drive.

During the by-election campaign for Joseph McGuinness in South Longford in May 1917, Michael stayed in the Greville Arms in Longford, a hotel run by the Kiernan family. Here he met the four attractive Kiernan girls – all of whom were in some way involved with their brother, Larry, in running the hotel, the bar, grocery and hardware shop, bakery and undertaking business. He took an instant liking to Helen but she was friendly with Paul McGovern; later when his attachment to Susan Killeen had ended he would pursue Helen.

Back in Dublin, Michael threw himself fully into his work at the National Aid office. Because of the many calls on the inadequate funds, especially by mid-June with more men released, there was a strain on the resources, and seeing so much poverty and unemployment he became more convinced that self-government was necessary. Kathleen Clarke had entrusted him with the names of the countrywide IRB contacts which her husband Tom had given her. This 'gave him the leeway to get ahead,' she says; furthermore 'he had the ability and the force and the enthusiasm and drive that very few men had, to work on that'.[3]

Kathleen Clarke had also requested Cathal Brugha's cooperation in the strengthening of the IRB. Despite her argument that more members of the IRB had participated in the Rising than any other body, and that the majority of the executed men were IRB men, she failed to receive Brugha's assistance. Not only that, but, she maintains, he set out to destroy it. 'I have decided the IRB must go!' he exclaimed one day as he stood in front of her and banged the table.[4]

Collins, on the other hand, believed in the secrecy principle which the brotherhood upheld – a principle which he maintained had carried them far. He belonged to the Tom Clarke/Seán MacDermott school of thought, which believed that physical force would be the surest method of getting the British authorities to accede to Irish self-government. He maintained that the Irish Volunteers and the IRB should work in tandem. Being on the IRB Supreme Council, on the Volunteer Provisional Executive and on the National Aid board helped him to become acquainted with men and women throughout Ireland who would one day become part of the 'great movement'.

Éamon de Valera, commandant at Boland's Mills during the 1916 Rising and already an acknowledged leader in Lewes jail, was returned as the Sinn Féin candidate on 10 July 1917, for the east Clare constituency.

As more and more prisoners were released, Collins' workload increased. He moved to more suitable office premises at 32 Bachelor's Walk (premises he used up until the Truce).

Vaughan's Hotel, Parnell Square, was the venue for a meeting of minds on many a night. Here Collins met Harry Boland, a young IRB activist who was also a member of the Volunteers, Sinn Féin and the GAA. Collins and Boland got on well; Boland had boundless energy and was enthusiastic and unselfish.

William T. Cosgrave, another survivor of 1916, won the Kilkenny by-election in August. Shortly afterwards, under the Defence of the Realm Act (DORA), the authorities saw a method of countering the disaffection by making widespread arrests. Three important leaders and close friends of Collins

– Austin Stack, Fionán Lynch and Thomas Ashe – were arrested in August and joined some forty others in Mountjoy Jail. They went on hunger-strike for political status and in an effort to break them, force-feeding was introduced. On 25 September Ashe was carried back to his cell, unconscious. Soon he was dead.

His funeral was used by uniformed Volunteers, Cumann na mBan and Sinn Féin members to mount a pageant of loyalty and solidarity. After the 'Last Post' had sounded, Collins, in military uniform, stepped forward and above the grave of his dead friend addressed the large assembly. As the crowds moved away, Collins stood, and wept bitterly. 'I grieve perhaps as no one else grieves,' he wrote afterwards to Hannie.[5]

From now on the mood of the country changed. Collins embarked on a nationwide campaign of meetings and speeches. He threw himself totally into whipping up recruits for the cause. 'You have no idea of how busy I've been,' he wrote to Hannie on 8 October. 'For about a fortnight I've been up almost alternate nights.'[6]

Totally committed to separatism and disagreeing with Arthur Griffith's dual monarchy concept, Collins was, however, aware of the power of Sinn Féin. He urged the IRB to support de Valera for the Sinn Féin presidency at the October Convention (Ard Fheis). De Valera was duly elected and Collins was elected director of organisation.

In March 1918 Collins was selected adjutant-general of the Volunteers, responsible for organising both disciplinary and training procedures. As well as continuing to travel and organise throughout Ireland, Mick became a periodic weekender at Sam Maguire's London flat to discuss with him and other IRB men the opening of channels for the procurement of armaments for Ireland. Meanwhile, on both sides of the Irish sea, he continued to spread his net, accumulating information about the movements of members of British intelligence, often seeking the assistance of women to explore avenues discreetly.

Since March 1917 he had been indirectly receiving copies of reports emanating from Dublin Castle, British military headquarters in Ireland. Ned (Éamon) Broy was employed at detective headquarters in Dublin Castle with, among other duties, the daily task of typing detective reports on the countrywide movements of Sinn Féin members. Broy would slip in an extra sheet of carbon. The third copy he discreetly gave to a Sinn Féin member who in turn passed it to Michael Collins.

When Collins first met Ned Broy, Broy outlined the inner workings of the Castle, its system and its training technique. The police were divided into six divisions, with the G Division responsible for nationalist movements. This division had a countrywide network of 'eyes and ears', its men filtering the daily activities of the nation – from railways to shops, police stations to ports.

In the early days of 1918 Collins recruited other national-minded detectives such as Joe Kavanagh and James Mac-Namara, who worked in the Castle. By this time most released prisoners had been absorbed into communities so there was little need for paid staff in the National Aid office. Collins had the freedom to pursue his ambition of full-time organiser of the cause of independence. Volunteers could drop into his office at 32 Bachelor's Walk – Volunteers such as Liam Tobin, intelligence officer to the Dublin Brigade. Harry Boland's tailor shop in Middle Abbey Street also became a centre where information was dropped, to be passed on to Mick. The two great friends would one day be rivals for the love of one young woman.

The Pulse of the Secret Service

One weekend in March 1918 Mick went to Longford with Harry Boland. He stayed in the Greville Arms, as he had done many times, and was entertained by the Kiernan sisters. Harry was courting the slim, vivacious, Kitty Kiernan at the time. Though her kind disposition charmed Mick, his friendship with Harry compelled him to keep her at arm's length. He found the lively-minded Helen most receptive to his views and hoped to win her affections, although she was friendly with solicitor Paul McGovern. Another sister Maud had been courted before his death by Mick's friend, Thomas Ashe. Mick's relationship with Susan Killeen was now more on a friendship basis with 'the cause' being the focal point. His current girlfriend was Sinn Féin sympathiser Madeline (Dilly) Dicker, whose sister Clare had worked in the British Post Office with him. Susan had found another boyfriend to take Mick's place. However, her place of work, P. S. O'Hegarty's bookshop on Dawson Street, was already among Collins' dispatch centres.

After Mass at Legga, near Granard, on this cold, March Sunday, Mick delivered a fiery speech condemning conscription and 'the raiding of private houses for the purpose of seizing old guns'. He urged that all young men should emulate the 'noble martyrs' of 1916 who put their own country first – they should join the Irish Volunteers and 'defend their rifles with their lives'.[1]

That evening he returned to Dublin; a few days later he headed for Limerick, then Cork, on organisational work. On 2 April he was confronted on Brunswick Street by detectives O'Brien and Bruton. He was, he wrote in his diary:

> ... detained in Brunswick Street for a few hours in a filthy, ill-ventilated cell ... Removed to Bridewell at 3.15 – 3.30. Cab accompanied by uniformed policeman, two detectives

(Smith & Wharton). The latter asked me how everything in the South was – showing they had been observing my weekend movements. Learned later on in the evening that as a matter of fact I had unknowingly slipped them at Kingsbridge on the previous night.

At 6 o'clock the following morning he was 'rudely awakened', and told to dress. He was escorted to Longford by train, and met at the station by quite a number of friends. During his trial he protested to the judge that he had been kidnapped in Dublin by an 'unlawful and immoral authority'. His plea was overruled. He was charged with having made a speech at Legga 'likely to cause disaffection' and remanded to the assizes to be held in July. Meanwhile, he was sent to Sligo jail. In line with Volunteer policy he did not seek bail.

On 11 April, Helen Kiernan visited Michael and gave him all the news of Granard. He was delighted to see her. He persuaded her to stay in town overnight so that she could visit him again next day. After a 'very bad night's sleep' he recorded he had 'the pleasure of seeing' Helen again. She promised to pay a return visit. 'All the people in Granard have always been very nice and kind to me,' he wrote in his journal.

(Some time later, to Michael's disappointment, Helen became engaged to Paul McGovern. He went to her in desperation and pleaded with her not to go through with the marriage but eventually became resigned to the situation.)

In his diary of 10 April he noted, 'Here alone I am in a state of appalling loneliness with the blackest despair in my heart. Of course the reason for my sadness and loneliness is the thought of the work I might be doing ...'[2]

In his letter to Hannie on 10 April, he said he was 'anxious to know what Lloyd George has done about conscription for this country. If he goes for it – well he's ended!'[3] He was unaware that on the previous day Lloyd George had introduced his Manpower Bill in parliament and extended conscription to Ireland. This became law on 16 April. The Irish Parliamentary Party, which for some time had lacked the support of a large section of the Irish people, withdrew from Westminster, thereby playing into the hands of Sinn Féin. The separatist bodies agreed that their members would put up bail so that the imprisoned men could be free to fight the conscription issue. Collins was among the first to be freed on bail.

Mick headed for Granard. Word went ahead of him and the local Volunteers assembled to give him 'a royal welcome' as he drove through the streets. His visit to the Kiernan sisters was short. Around the dining-room table he told the story of his time in jail and Kitty brought him up to date on their mutual friend, Harry Boland, and on activities in Dublin.

Pressure of organisational work forced him to pick up the threads quickly in the fight against conscription. Though 180,000 Irish men had already volunteered for service in the British army, it was clear that compulsion would not work. Men flocked to the Irish Volunteers. Women joined Cumann na mBan in large numbers. Anti-conscription rallies and protests took on more impetus countrywide. On the night of 17 May and throughout the next day police scoured the country and arrested many of the senior officers of Sinn Féin and the Volunteers on the pretext that they were involved in what became known as 'the German Plot'. Though there was no organised plot for a 'rising' with German aid, the authorities used the excuse as a ploy to take the leaders out of circulation.

Collins was annoyed by the arrests. If British intelligence were monitoring the movements of the separatists, why not turn the tables and monitor British intelligence? Dublin Castle detective Joe Kavanagh arrived one day at Capel Street Public Library and handed the librarian Thomas Gay the names of key people listed for arrest. Gay passed the list to Harry Boland. Mick Collins had already received a warning from the young Castle police clerk, Ned Broy, but now he had a list with his own name on it.

During a Sinn Féin Executive meeting held on the night of 18 May 1918, Mick advised certain 'listed' members to go 'on the run'. He told Kathleen Clarke she was 'on the list', but as she had three young children she said she was 'neither temperamentally nor physically fit for such a life'. She decided to let fate decide. That night she was watched; she was arrested next morning and sent to Holloway Prison, where she was kept until February 1919.[4]

After the meeting Collins headed for Seán McGarry's house to warn him, but already the raid had begun. Collins, helpless, stood with onlookers as McGarry was taken away. When they left he went in and slept in McGarry's bed. 'I knew it would be the safest bed in Dublin,' he told Ernie O'Malley.

Arrests such as these helped the anti-conscription lobby, boosted Sinn Féin's political campaign, continued to swell Volunteer enlistment and helped the imprisoned Arthur Griffith to win a seat in the Cavan by-election.

Already Mick Collins had begun to nudge his way into the laneways of the secret service in Ireland, by means of his informants in the heart of Dublin Castle. When in May 1918 the Sinn Féin leaders were arrested because of their opposition to conscription, he began to put his faith more and more in revolutionary methods.

In the same month Mick asked his old friend Joe O'Reilly to join him in his work. O'Reilly would be courier, clerk, valet, cook and buffer for his many moods; cheerfully he would carry out detective work and negotiate with Mick the snares of the British secret service.

Mick kept in regular contact with his friend, Austin Stack, who, with Fionán Lynch, Ernest Blythe and others, was in Belfast jail. Stack would write to Mick via Mick's cousin,

Nancy O'Brien, who worked in the GPO.

Although public gatherings had been banned, Sinn Féin and their allies defied the British government and held 1,800 rallies countrywide on 18 August 1918. These rallies, cooperatively organised by Cumann na mBan, the Volunteers, Sinn Féin and Gaelic League members, set the tone of separatism. 'The conscription proposals are to my liking,' Collins wrote to Hannie, 'as I think they will end well for Ireland.'[5] With sheer methodical detail he correlated the data of every Volunteer company, every battalion, every brigade countrywide – their distance and direction from the nearest town or village, the names and addresses of their officers and whether or not they were in jail. In order to assemble this information he needed a vast network of couriers. These were mostly women, such as Máire Comerford, Leslie Price (who later married Tom Barry) and Sheila Humphreys. Up and down the country they travelled, helping with affiliation forms containing inventories of the arms and equipment, which were scant and obtained mainly by raids on barracks or police personnel. The forms included details of stretchers, bandages, signalling equipment, even pikes.[6]

Despite his busy schedule Mick found time to write to comrades in prison, often sending some little surprise. 'I know you don't smoke, but I remember you saying you liked candies,' he wrote to Kathleen Clarke, sending a package to her in Holloway Prison.

Mick knew he had to avoid arrest at all costs. He moved his office to a cellar known as the 'dugout' in St Ita's in Ranelagh – the school founded by Pádraig Pearse. From here he began to conduct his intelligence business. When he sent Ernie O'Malley to London on IRB work, he was annoyed to find out that Cathal Brugha had men in readiness in London to assassinate British cabinet ministers, should conscription be enforced. O'Malley disliked Brugha's tactics and he knew that Mick did also.

In July, with the sanction of GHQ, Mick asked Piaras Béaslaí to become editor of the secret journal, *An tÓglach*. Mick wrote 'Notes on Organisation' for *An tÓglach*, and was involved in its publication, as well as distribution and subscriptions. Copies found their way to remote corners of Ireland, in bags of flour, in women's handbags or inside their coats. Mick's personal secretary Sinéad Mason knew his every quirk. She knew when he wanted something done now that it was 'now!' But she also knew his kind streak and that he valued her judgement.

In November a change came with the signing of the armistice ending the Great War. Volunteers and Cumann na mBan who had worked so unitedly against conscription now had time to turn their attentions more intensely towards the fight for independence.

Lloyd George called a general election, and immediately the Sinn Féin machine prepared to fight. The British parliament granted the parliamentary franchise to all women over thirty, so in this 1918 election women would have a more active part. Both women and men in Sinn Féin courted women voters' newly acquired power, and promised (somewhat unrealistically) that 'as in the past, so in the future the womenfolk of the Gael shall have high place in the Councils of a freed Gaelic nation'.[7]

As many of Sinn Féin members were in jail it fell on leaders outside, such as Mick Collins, Harry Boland, Diarmuid O'Hegarty, Fr O'Flanagan, Jennie Wyse-Power and Hanna Sheehy Skeffington, to select candidates and promote their campaign. 'The candidates who did face the electorate when Collins and Boland had finished with the lists were all staunch Republicans.'[8]

Sinn Féin nominated two women to stand for election – Constance Markievicz (who was in jail) for Dublin and Winifred Carey (who had been a nurse in the GPO in 1916) for Belfast.

Sinn Féin enjoyed a great victory at the expense of the Irish Parliamentary Party. Constance Markievicz was the first women elected to the House of Commons but even when released she, like the other Sinn Féin candidates, was loyal to her election pledge and refused to take her seat. Instead the First Dáil was convened in Dublin in January 1919. (Winifred Carey was unsuccessful in the election.)

Mick and Harry Boland were absent for the first session of the First Dáil on 21 January 1919. They were involved in securing the escape of Éamon de Valera from Lincoln Jail. On Mick's return he found that Dan Breen and some Volunteer comrades, in an attempt to get explosives, had killed two policemen in Soloheadbeg, County Tipperary, on the same day as the Dáil's first assembly. Mick was now convinced that 'all ordinary peaceful means are ended and we shall be taking the only alternative actions in a short while now'.[9]

Collins had been appointed minister of home affairs in the opening Dáil, while Cathal Brugha was elected acting president. At the second Dáil meeting on 1 April 1919, de Valera was elected president – prime minister (príomh aire) of Dáil Éireann. Next day he named his cabinet, which included Michael Collins as minister of finance (he relinquished his home affairs portfolio).

As well as his many tasks, he now had to get accustomed to ministerial duties. Soon his waking hours would eat into his time for sleep. Despite this he found time to drop a few lines to his sister Helena (a nun, Sister Celestine, in England) to tell her about the busy week for Dáil members:

> ... it has been an historical one for very often we are actors in events that have very much more meaning and consequence than we realise ... The elected representatives of the people have definitely turned their backs on the old order and the developments are sure to be interesting ... We go from success to success in our own guerrilla way. Escapes of prisoners, raids against the enemy, etc.[10]

After a few months of relatively unrestricted movement, he was now truly 'on the run'. An order had been issued for his arrest owing to his failure to attend the spring assizes in Derry to answer the charge for which a year earlier he had been given bail.

Intelligence-gathering Continues

Michael Collins was preoccupied with his many different roles but one of his most steadfast resolves was to crack the British secret service machine. His intelligence-gathering had already begun to bear fruit, with the help of men such as MacNamara, Kavanagh, Broy and David Neligan working for him from within Dublin Castle. He acknowledged the British espionage system as being 'the most efficient in the world' and knew that he had to have men and women to counteract it.

One night in April 1919 Mick asked Broy to get him into Dublin Castle. 'Get me into Headquarters,' he said, 'I have to see what the buggers are up to.'

Detectives were asleep upstairs, and Broy had taken the precaution of locking their dormitory door from outside. Broy led Collins and Seán Nunan, who accompanied them, to a small locked room on the top floor. With his duplicate key he opened the door and gave Mick the key to lock themselves in. Here the two spent several hours among the secret documents, making notes from the many reports. In one report, Mick found himself described as a man who 'comes of a brainy Cork family'; at this he laughed heartily.[1]

Mick's cousin, Nancy O'Brien, had returned to Dublin early in 1916 with her friends Susan Killeen and Dolly Brennan. In 1918, as an employee of the British government, she was summoned one day by Sir James MacMahon and given the job of handling the Castle secret coded messages, because of her efficiency and because Sir James wanted somebody he could trust. When Mick heard the news he gleefully shouted, 'In the name of Jasus how did they [the British] ever get an empire!' But he knew he had something gold couldn't buy. He knew Nancy well and valued her resilience and daring.

During many a lunch-hour Nancy snatched quiet moments

in the privacy of the post office lavatory to copy decoded messages which she then hid in the bodice of her dress or elsewhere on her person. This was done without thought for the risk to herself. In her Glasnevin flat she would sort her messages and clarify further points before passing the messages on to Mick.

This hardworking, brave young woman took many chances but would at times get angry with Mick for taking her for granted. One evening he raged because he maintained that there was an important document that she should have seen which referred to warders. He wanted to know its contents. All she saw, she told him, was some rubbish about 'Angelus bells' and some admirer talking about 'the light glinting in her hair'.

'What sort of an eejit are you anyway?' he cried. 'That's the message I'm looking for.' In an instant he had figured it out – the warders change at six o'clock and our target man will be in his room when the light goes on! Tears filled Nancy's eyes. Then she exploded and told him what he could do with his messages.

It was well after midnight when Nancy was awakened by pebbles thrown at her window. Mick, defying the curfew, had come to apologise. 'I'm sorry for what happened, I shouldn't have said it. I'm under the most terrible strain,' he said and as he turned to leave he placed a small paper bag on the garden wall. 'Here's a little present for you.' Back into the night he went, this man 'on the run', leaving a bag of bull's-eyes for Nancy.[2]

Over the next few years Nancy would continue her detective work for Mick. 'I used to get private correspondence for him, leaving it each morning at one of his many depots. I copied telegrams in our office at Upper O'Connell Street [then Sackville Street] ... telegrams for detective police – Lord French and others.' Mick had agents 'in the GPO who gave him each week the code to these private telegrams.'[3]

Jim Walsh from Cork, a high official in the Post Office, was one of those in a position to obtain the weekly code. This code he discreetly dropped into Harry Boland's tailor shop for Mick. Piaras Béaslaí then suggested that his cousin Lily Mernin, a typist at Dublin Castle, might be in a position to help Mick with information. During her first interview with Mick, Lily told him things 'which he carefully noted down on sheets and then concealed them in his socks'. He suggested to her methods of obtaining further information, including the deciphering of Castle carbon paper.

From then on Piaras Béaslaí received documents from Lily every few days which he dispatched to Mick, as director of intelligence of the Volunteers. Mick gave Lily a key to a house in Clonliffe Road. Over the next few years she would let herself in, type up records of her deciphering and place her work in a sealed envelope which Mick later collected. She compiled a list of officers, many disguised as civilians, using pseudonyms and living outside barracks. This list, regularly updated, Béaslaí passed on to Collins. Never throughout the period did Lily meet any of Collins' intelligence officers nor any of the inhabitants of the house on Clonliffe Road. All had their own schedules and worked independently within Mick's intelligence network.[4]

From as early as 1917 Siobhán Creedon, who was employed as an official at Mallow Post Office in County Cork, had been engaged in active work for the Volunteers. In 1919 she secured valuable information in regard to British plans, which was promptly passed to Richard Mulcahy. The RIC used the telegraph system for urgent business, and often transmitted messages by cable. The 'key supplied regularly by Mick Collins, Director of Intelligence' meant that Siobhán could decipher the messages and send the information back to Mick and pass relevant information to the Cork brigades.

This method was used also in Cork City by Josephine Marchmount, head of civilian clerks and typists (a staff of

25), in the 6th Division at Cork Military Barracks. She was therefore in a senior pivotal position with access to information on most internal activities of the 6th Division including the activities of Captain Webb, chief officer to Major General Sir Peter Strickland, commander of British forces in Munster and the counties of Kilkenny and Wexford. Josephine, being of good standing, was absolutely trusted by the authorities. Her father had been a constable in the RIC and a friend of Captain Webb's. Her husband was killed in the Great War.

After her husband's death she retained custody of her younger son, Gerald, but her oldest son, Reggie was placed in the custody of her mother-in-law in South Wales. Josephine expressed her desire, to get Reggie back, to a friend. This information got to the ears of Seán Hegarty and Florrie O'Donoghue of the Cork No. 1 Brigade. Florrie contacted Mick Collins, who immediately saw how valuable she could be, and set about organising an offer she couldn't refuse. After a lapse of time Mick put Florrie in touch with the London IRA and with Pat O'Donoghue in Manchester. Soon Florrie and Jack Cody were on the boat to England. The plan didn't go smoothly, but after much manoeuvring, aided by a Liverpool Volunteer Seán Phelan, Reggie (with his helpers) was on a ferry to Cork and reunited with his mother.

Henceforth, Josephine Marchmount would be an intelligence agent. On many occasions she supplied information about locations earmarked for raids, names of Sinn Féin and Volunteers on the military's wanted list, and most important of all, names of paid informers – data of immense value to the three Cork brigades. She was in a position to confirm troop movements and this in turn helped Volunteers 'on the run'. Josephine, in such a key position, worked in tandem with Nora Wallace. Nora in her shop in St Augustine Street became the keeper of a police cipher key and with their contacts in Cork city post office 'wire messages were regularly decoded' thus aiding Florrie O'Donoghue and his intelligence team to keep 'a step ahead of their enemies'. Intelligence work done by both Josephine and Nora went undetected throughout the war and was regarded by Florrie O'Donoghue as of equivalent value 'to a strong column of men'. (After hostilities ended, Josephine married Florrie O'Donoghue.)[5]

Countrywide reports of ill-treatment by the Royal Irish Constabulary (RIC) of citizens suspected of being involved in separatist movements were daily reaching GHQ. A decree of social ostracism on the RIC was passed by the members of Dáil Éireann and introduced to the public by de Valera in a strongly worded statement. It was left to Mick Collins to neutralise the intelligence work of the members of this force who acted as agents for the British espionage system.

Through all this time, Mick wove his way through Dublin on an old rusty bike. During business hours he crossed the city, briefcase in hand, his businessman cover helping him to escape detection.

The intensification of the war meant that Mick had to devise means of detecting those who were trying to detect him. In July, 1919, the Squad, later known as 'Mick's twelve apostles', was recruited and paid as an assassination team. This group of men, under the command initially of Michael McDonnell and later of Patrick Daly, was selected from the intelligence department for dangerous and difficult jobs.

British spies and intelligence officers in mufti mingled with other shoppers and business people on Dublin's Grafton Street and Dame Street. Lily Mernin would saunter up and down these streets on the arm of Frank Saurin or Tom Cullen (two of Mick's principal intelligence officers), ostensibly window-shopping. Her task was to identify these Castle intelligence agents for the Squad. Lily took great risks but remained undetected throughout the period of hostilities.

Mick was regularly in touch with several women including Brigid Lyons (later Lyons-Thornton), a medical student who worked as an undercover agent. Mingled with her college notes she often held messages, sometimes in code, for Mick. As a Cumann na mBan member, Brigid had been arrested for her participation in the 1916 Rising. The early months of 1917 found her with Collins and others electioneering for her uncle Joe McGuinness, as Sinn Féin candidate for South Longford. Especially from 1919 onwards, Brigid was a dispatch carrier for Collins, often acting as a conduit between him and people in the Longford and the Galway area. (She had begun her medical studies UCG, and later qualified in UCD). The intelligence work done by women such as Brigid and women working in post offices, in railway stations, in boarding houses and the many who were in a position to observe the activities of British agents meant that Collins could coordinate all the information. At meetings with the Squad, movements were worked out and tactics were put in place to deal with the regular harassment and terrorisation of citizens. Piaras Béaslaí recalls that for Mick 'office work was almost as important as outside work'.[6] He certainly had an aptitude for the detailed and methodical handling of information.

Women Linchpin in Espionage

In mid-1919, Mick was appointed president of the Supreme Council of the IRB. At this period tensions with Cathal Brugha came to the fore. 'I'm fed up,' he wrote to Austin Stack, who was in jail. 'Things are not going very smoothly ... All sorts of miserable little undercurrents are working and the effect is anything but good.' He was determined that no secret organisation should undermine the Dáil; he saw the activities of the IRB and of the Volunteers as aiding the political process to achieve its aims.

The departure of de Valera for America meant that more responsibility for the Volunteer movement and Sinn Féin was thrown upon Mick and his comrades. In June 1919, though himself opposed to the move, he had helped Dev to fulfil his ambition to go on a fundraising and awareness mission, by arranging for his travel incognito to America, via Liverpool.

As minister of finance, Mick had prepared a prospectus for the fundraising which would be required in the struggle for independence and the construction of a new independent state. The Dáil had agreed to float a national loan along the lines of a scheme organised by the Fenians but de Valera and Collins had disagreed on some of the details.

In de Valera's absence, Arthur Griffith was acting president, and Mick as minister of finance was in constant consultation with him. According to Piaras Béaslaí: 'It was about this time, while Collins and Griffith were being drawn together, that Cathal Brugha began to be estranged from Collins'. Brugha now advocated 'extreme and drastic action against the English government,' and wanted cabinet members assassinated. Mick opposed this scheme; he could not in this case see the ends justifying the means. He argued that British cabinet ministers, unlike secret service men,

50

could be replaced, that 'intelligence data carried in the head had greater significance!'

Mick was director of intelligence of the Volunteers and continued to act as adjutant-general and director of organisation, as well as being minister of finance. He filled all these demanding roles from three offices: Cullenswood House in Ranelagh, Bachelor's Walk and a finance department office at 6 Harcourt Street.

Much of his time was absorbed by the national loan; the work for this was done at Number 6 Harcourt Street. His energy and vitality inspired those around him. He frowned at any laxity during working hours, and did not permit swearing in front of ladies. Once he held Desmond Fitzgerald's head under the tap for refusing to admit Nancy O'Brien to the office. Decorum was important; ladies should get lunch at a proper time and always be respected. For himself there was never enough time and he would hastily devour sandwiches fetched by Joe O'Reilly.

At this time Robert Barton wrote to a mutual friend, Moya Llewelyn Davies, that 'Mick is very well & very hearty, a tower of strength & by no means the wild extremist he is supposed to be. The only extreme things about him are daring and determination.'[1] Mick had known Moya when he lived in London and through Batt O'Connor, a relative of hers, she had already sent some vital information to Mick about how Lloyd George was determined to quell what he called the 'terrorists' in Ireland.[2]

In mid-1919 Mick's great friend and comrade Harry Boland also departed for America to help de Valera to raise funds and create awareness. The two had grown close when other Sinn Féin leaders were in jail: they were around the same age and wrestled and played hurley together. On Sundays they would often head for Granard to stay in the Greville Arms Hotel. Away from the hectic city life Mick enjoyed the relaxed atmosphere and the companionship of the Kiernan sisters. Harry Boland was in love with Kitty. There was the odd game of tennis, and under the vigilant protection of local scouts the house parties in their rented country cottage were always a time of laughter, music, dancing and conversation. Mick was a good dancer, and in particular he enjoyed the céilís. But above all he loved the countryside, the long walks, the stimulating conversation with the Kiernan girls and their brother.

At all times Collins acted contrary to the authorities' perception of a wanted man. He dressed and acted normally despite their efforts to seek him out and in fact it was this normality and daring that saw him through. In the summer of 1919 his sister Katie (Sheridan) boarded the Mayo train for Dublin. Intelligence men had her under observation from the outset and sent news ahead that a woman clad in a brown gaberdine coat was on her way to meet her brother, Michael Collins. Katie had been ill and was cold and pale. A friend of hers, whom she met at Athlone station, insisted that Katie take a loan of her fur coat and give her the gaberdine instead.

At midnight when the train arrived in Dublin station a military presence was evident. Passengers were ordered to remain seated; there was to be a search.

Mick had asked Joe O'Reilly to meet Katie at the station. As people waited on the platform, Joe looked around, saw Mick standing behind him, then watched as Mick pushed forward and asked a porter, 'What's the hold-up?' When a British officer replied that it was that 'damned Collins again' he told the officer that he had already been held up twice that day because of that blackguard! Then he spotted Katie. He told the officer he was meeting that passenger; she was ill. The lady did not resemble the description of the lady they were looking for in a brown gaberdine. The British officer told him to go ahead. Mick stepped on the train, politely took her hand and O'Reilly, in gentlemanly fashion, linked
52

her arm and escorted her out, with Mick at heel, still muttering and shaking his head. They walked past some military men who stood by while their comrades continued to search the train.[3]

Each morning O'Reilly met the incoming boat at the North Wall. Gelignite from the Welsh coalfields packed in tin trunks and rifles in wicker baskets and timber boxes marked 'China – Fragile' were put aside by reliable handlers 'for collection'. Sailors, workmen or women returning from a visit to relations regularly walked past the military with revolvers and ammunition tucked discreetly into their bags – arms that eventually found their way to Collins and his men.

The photo held by police was totally unlike the real Michael Collins. In *The Police Gazette or Hue-And-Cry*, under 'Apprehensions Sought', a description and sometimes a photograph 'of persons who are wanted' was given. It stated, 'If any of them be found they should be arrested and a telegram sent to Head Quarters'. Michael Collins is described as 'M. P. (Dublin City and Cork W. R.), age 28, height 5 ft. 11, complexion fresh'.[4] Not much to go on.

Mick's intelligence from Dublin Castle continued to improve. In July 1919, when his information on Detective Sergeant Smith exposed how close 'Dog Smith' had got to capturing him, Mick decided he had to be cut down. Though Collins has come to be regarded in some quarters as a ruthless orchestrator of killings – he is not known ever to have killed anyone himself – there is evidence from some people who worked closely with him that ordering killings filled him with tension and anxiety. He would pace the floor until news was brought to him that the killing had taken place.

Kathleen McKenna recalls an occasion during a discussion on spies, when a young lady who believed she would please him exclaimed, 'Of course, every spy should be shot'. Angrily, he turned on her and 'gave his emphatic view of the conditions of judgement and punishment.'[5]

His method of secrecy and segregation of each department worked very effectively. He informed Tobin, Cullen and Frank Thornton which other agents they needed to meet but gave no further information. For instance, they were unaware that he travelled one day a week to Thomas Gay's house in Clontarf to meet Kavanagh, Broy and MacNamara and to collect documents compiled by Lily Mernin.

Guerrilla warfare had begun but as yet only on a small scale. In early August 1919 Mick travelled to the closing stages of a week-long training camp in west Cork and on his return he recommended to brigades countrywide to set up similar training camps. The flying columns were the result.

He was as hard on himself as he was on others. 'I'll be a slave to nothing,' he told his sister Katie on his decision to abandon his heavy smoking, because he was 'becoming a slave to cigarettes'.[6]

From 21 August 1919 Mick's burden increased with the public announcement that the Dáil had sanctioned a national loan of £250,000 to be raised in Ireland and $5,000,000 in America. Dáil Éireann was suppressed on 12 September, and on that day Mick was in his minister of finance office on the upper floor of 6 Harcourt Street. Shortly after midday he heard a commotion downstairs; a raid was in progress. He opened the back window so that he could slide down a drain-pipe but the pipe was out of reach. He handed his revolver and some of his writings, including his handwritten journal from his time in Sligo jail, to his secretary, Sinéad Mason, snatched documents to lob into the specially converted secret closet and was halfway to the door when an inspector from G Division walked in. He didn't know Mick but confronted him and asked to see the papers he was holding.

'What's it got to do with you? A nice job you have, spying on your fellow countrymen,' said Mick casually, and he brushed past out the door. Once out of sight on the landing he headed upstairs to the caretaker's apartments at the top of the house, through the skylight, on to the roof and across to the roof of the Ivanhoe Hotel. Here he waited until the two military lorries of soldiers armed with rifles and bayonets 'together with a large detachment of G Division detectives' had departed. Over an hour later he returned to his desk and a room full of scattered documents, to discover that Pádraig O'Keeffe, assistant secretary, Sinn Féin, and Ernest Blythe, TD, had been arrested.[7]

The next night Detective Inspector Daniel Hoey was shot dead outside the door of police headquarters in Brunswick Street. Hoey had been responsible for the raid, had worked 'with zeal', according to Mick, 'to secure victims for execution,' after the 1916 Rising and had continued to spy 'on his fellow countrymen'.[8]

To counteract the clampdown by the authorities on advertising the national loan in the newspapers. Mick arranged a Movietone mini-film for the American market. It depicted a bond-signing outside St Enda's with a number of people including Kathleen Clarke, Nora Connolly and Pádraig Pearse's mother purchasing bonds from Mick and Diarmuid O'Hegarty. This helped to sell more bonds, gave Mick a high profile in Sinn Féin circles, and added to the allure of the wanted man who continued to evade capture. In the film he wore a hat, which he never wore as he hastened about the city. His friend Harry Boland in the United States was amused: 'That film of yourself and Hegarty selling Bonds brought tears to me eyes. Gee Boy! You are some movie actor. Nobody could resist buying a bond and we having such a handsome minister of finance.'[9]

The authorities wanted Collins in their grip, held, not dead. He had many close shaves. During the early days of January 1920 all his haunts were raided and it was only thanks to MacNamara's tip-offs from the inner sanctums of the

Castle and Mick's teams outside that he was able to remain ahead of the posse. A detective called Redmond came too close for comfort and finally Collins ordered him to be shot, on 21 January, 1920. On 25 January a reward of £10,000 was offered by the British authorities for information leading to the killers, and 'especially to the man who issued the order.'[10] No one ever claimed this reward.

Martial law came into force in Dublin on 23 February 1920. This made it 'like a city of the dead', Mick said to his friend Dónal Hales. 'It is the English way of restoring peace to this country.'[11] Offices at Number 6 Harcourt Street were now being raided so often that Mick instructed Batt O'Connor to buy Number 76, which was for sale. O'Connor, a builder, fitted a room with a concealed hiding place and an escape route through the skylight. Sir Hamar Greenwood, chief secretary at Dublin Castle, had decided to implement a hardline policy because undercover agents and RIC men had been targeted by Collins' Squad without mercy. Greenwood's men now had instructions to retaliate.

After an RIC constable was shot in Cork, a group of men with blackened faces stormed the home of Tomás MacCurtain, lord mayor of Cork, on the night of 20 March 1920, and shot him dead in front of his wife and children. Evidence later revealed that the killers were assisted by the RIC. The episode angered and upset Collins, as he and MacCurtain had been friends since they were interned in Frongoch.

Collins in turn felt that he and his comrades had no option but to 'adopt more extreme measures'. More extreme, he said, 'than would have been the case had we had the active, united support of the whole people. I am making no apology for what we did in these succeeding years – I hope merely to explain the necessity which drove us'.[12]

In May 1920 Mick's friend Harry Boland returned from America for a month's break. There was a boisterous reunion.

Though the two men had corresponded regularly it gave Mick the opportunity to catch up on the news from America. Harry went to Granard to meet Kitty Kiernan, to whom he was more than ever attached. One weekend in early June, Joe Hyland drove Mick and Harry down to Granard, where they danced at a céilí. Mick certainly was fond of Kitty, but she was Harry's girl.

In Dublin on 17 June, Harry spent a few hours talking business with Fr O'Flanagan, vice-president of Sinn Féin, then popped into a tobacconist and scribbled a note to Kitty: '... I need not say how truly wonderful my few days holiday were to me. I feel, however, that I treated you rather unfairly in keeping you from your slumbers ... If I could only be with you I would indeed try to make you happy. It may be that I will come back soon again from overseas ... I long to be in Ireland, more so than ever that I have hopes to win the girl I love best in the world ...'[13]

On 25 June, Mick risked going to the North Wall with Kitty to comfort her as she bade a sad farewell to Harry. Harry's 'goodbye and best love' telegram to Kitty from Southampton reached her as he sailed across the Atlantic. Harry's love for Kitty was strong but later he had a rival for her affections.

To the young ladies who knew him, Mick Collins was a tall, dark, handsome man with sharp intellect and a mysterious aura. He had no difficulty in getting them to do intelligence work for him. If he had a sixth sense, they too appeared to have a sixth sense when he was in danger.

At this time his girlfriend was Dilly Dicker. Many a night he hid in the attic of her parents' Mountjoy Street guesthouse home while she played the piano in the parlour. Madeline, nicknamed Dilly by Mick, was born in 1899, to parents Alice Godfrey and Michael Dicker. Her grandparents were Sir John and Lady Godfrey of Glenflesk Castle, Killarney and Kilcolman Abbey, Cork. Her father, Michael Dicker, was an assistant commissioner in the valuation office of the British civil service but sympathetic to the cause. Mick felt that the civil service link also gave him good cover. Across the road in Mrs MacCarthy's, 44 Mountjoy Street, there was another safe house, where Mick, Harry Boland, J. J. Walsh and many others on the run slept. There was a prearranged signal between the two houses in case of a raid. Mrs MacCarthy would go to the door, look right and left, then give the all-clear by rearranging her curtains.

Dilly was light-hearted, musical, beautiful and full of bounce. She played the piano for the silent movies. Her personality appealed to Mick and she accepted that he had to duck in and out of her life as the occasion demanded. Mick was generally 'in great haste', but he crammed as much as he could into each day.

In the early days Dilly took messages to Liam Tobin and Tom Cullen about meeting times and places but as time progressed a romance blossomed. And just as Susan Killeen had entertained him with poetry, Dilly played the piano to ease his tired mind. She would also play the harp and zither in the background while Mick scribbled on his spiral notepad. Sometimes he was so exhausted that he would fall asleep on the chair.

During 1919 and 1920 when Mick was constantly on the run, he found periods of respite, mostly brief, in Dilly's tender arms. Although Mick was strong and forceful with his comrades, he was gentle, affectionate and kind to Dilly. It was a time when men respected women, and within the Volunteers there was an unspoken code that unless a couple was married it would be improper to engage in sex. 'The man who made a girl pregnant, if his identity became known, was ostracised as much as the girl herself,' according to Todd Andrews. 'Dignity was incorporated within the Volunteer code. We had principles and we all lived up to them. Mick Collins was no exception.' Within these parameters, relationships were romantic and gentle.[14]

58

In 1920, as romance blossomed between them, Dilly got deeper into helping Mick with intelligence. Aided by his men, Dilly would climb into one of the larger wickerwork mail baskets, which were pulled on a hand-truck. Covered with letters, she would be wheeled on to the mailboat and into the mail room, where she would emerge in a sorter's uniform – sorting of mail for Britain was done, at this time, on the boat. Letters destined for the British secret service would find their way into her handbag or her bosom, or inside her elastic-legged knickers. She would be met at the other side of the Irish Sea by a man or woman sent by Sam Maguire or Art O'Brien. Letters might sometimes be opened in London but she would usually bring them back to Dublin to be studied by Mick's sharp eye. On the return journey she would again extract from the mail baskets letters destined for Dublin Castle or for British agents who, Collins knew, were acting as businessmen at addresses throughout Dublin. The names of Mick's suspects became very familiar to Dilly.

Back in Dublin, very often out in Howth (in the flat rented by Susan Killeen, Nancy O'Brien and Dolly Brennan, all of whom worked in the city) Mick and his team would steam open the mail. If Mick felt that a response was needed to some communication, Dilly would insert that letter into the mail on her next trip. By this intelligence work, Dilly played an active part in shielding Mick from capture and also in opening the British secret service to him.

Dilly never came under suspicion as she possessed an innocent composure and was smart and pretty. She was in demand as a sitter for painters such as Augustus John and Leo Whelan, posing in guises such as 'Innocence' and 'The Shepherdess'.

One night the Auxiliaries pounced on Dilly's house. Mick made for his attic hideaway, while Dilly gently touched the piano keys. To the background strains of 'The Old Rustic Bridge by the Mill', the Auxies flung open doors and cupboards, scattered books, clothes baskets and bedlinen. Mick remained crouched above the concealed entrance for what seemed like hours, until Dilly gave the all-clear. Covered in dust and cobwebs he made for the opening, lost his balance and put his boot through the ceiling. His leap to safety brought peals of laughter from Dilly. Later that night he got Batt O'Connor to repair the damage – there would be no giveaways for next time. Two days later he arrived to see Dilly with a lucky boot charm in his pocket. They hugged and kissed, laughing when their eyes fell on where the hole had been.

Many a night Mick would arrive with a paper-fist of bull's-eyes, which they would savour on the tram to Dalkey as he headed out to meet Liam Tobin and Tom Cullen. The pair would sit at the front after Mick had a brief word with the driver, who always seemed to be 'one of ours'. One evening Dilly was startled to hear Mick mutter something about a raid. He edged discreetly towards the destination sign-box and calmly placed his revolver inside.

Dilly had a versatile musquash coat which she loved and which she practically wore to bed. She wore it when she went out to one of the picture houses to play the piano that accompanied the silent movies. She wore it when she went out with Mick. One day they were strolling down Sackville Street when Mick noticed a hold-up in the distance. Instantly he slid her his revolver and she slipped it into her pocket. But to his consternation and hers, the revolver careered through a hole in the pocket and clattered on the ground. With quick reflexes she grabbed it, linked his arm and the two ducked in through a shop and out of sight.

On another occasion he was on his way to meet some of 'the boys'. As they headed along Dawson Street he spotted some military approaching. In the busy street, he stopped a woman who pushed a pram and chatted to her. He admired the baby. 'Is it a boy or a girl?' he asked, as he bent forward

60

and slid his revolver under the covers.

Dilly lived with this intrigue and Mick showed his appreciation by bringing her little trinkets. Once he came in the side door of Number 30 Mountjoy Street in his usual lively manner and threw a tiny Bible charm on her lap as she sat playing the piano – a reminder of her forefathers, he said. On another occasion it was a miniature crucifix and rosary beads. He knew she had a casual approach to religion but he found consolation in it. He knew Dilly loved mementos, so whether they were religious or not he would on impulse buy a suitable trinket whenever he spotted one.[15]

Mick now worked as many hours as he could remain awake. He had contacts everywhere, in offices within the British establishment, in Scotland Yard, with workers on railways, in hotels, cross-channel boats and within the post office system. His cousin Nancy O'Brien constantly took risks to get messages to him. She knew him well by now, was familiar with his antics and accepted that his teasing was as much part of him as his impetuous gestures, movements and constant changes of expression.

While Mick and GHQ had embarked on a campaign in Dublin, the Volunteers countrywide had begun to intensify their campaign. Raids and arrests were commonplace and jails were becoming overcrowded. Brigades everywhere had men and women trained to shoot, to fight, to secure intelligence data and to avoid capture. Members of Cumann na mBan worked with the Volunteers, now generally known as the IRA (Irish Republican Army). To prop up the RIC, men were recruited in England, and with no specific training and little guidance arrived in Ireland in March 1920. These were nicknamed the Black and Tans. Then in autumn 1920 another hastily recruited group of ex-servicemen known as the Auxiliaries arrived in Ireland. Both groups were without military discipline. In the rapidly disintegrating administration the government's policy was to fight terror with terror. Field Marshal Henry Wilson had decided that a counter-murder policy was the answer to what he termed 'Sinn Féin murders'.

The Heart of British Intelligence

By the end of 1920 guerrilla warfare was prevalent country-wide, and gradually the IRA was adding to its scant supply of arms. Mick, in a letter to Dónal Hales, who was working for the cause in Italy, expressed anger that 'the enemy continues to be savage and ruthless, and innocent people are murdered and outraged daily'.[1]

In July 1920, Mick was saddened to hear of the arrest and ill-treatment of Tom Hales, Dónal's brother. Tom was hospitalised, then sentenced to penal servitude and held in Pentonville Prison until after the Treaty was signed.[2] Another good friend of Mick's, Terence MacSwiney, lord mayor of Cork, who had been arrested in August, went on hunger-strike in Brixton Prison, focusing world attention on the Irish cause. He died in October 1920 on the seventy-fifth day of his hunger strike. In the same month, Mick arranged the escape of his friends Austin Stack and Piaras Béaslaí from Manchester Jail.

As a reprisal for IRA killings of members of the British forces, Churchill pressed for capital punishment. On 1 November 1920, his policy was put into practice when Kevin Barry, an eighteen-year-old university student, was hanged in Mountjoy Jail. He had been captured after an IRA raid which left two British soldiers dead. Efforts failed to have Barry's sentence commuted and Collins also failed to arrange his escape from Mountjoy.

On 22 December 1919 Lloyd George with the 'Better Government of Ireland' Bill in the House of Commons had outlined proposals to 'set up two governments' – a separate government for north-east Ulster.

Because of constant raids, Mick moved office from Number 76, this time to a small two-storeyed house on Mespil Road with a gateway entrance. In the lace-curtained parlour he would work at his desk, his revolver beside him. A tunnel get-away was devised by Batt O'Connor. Only Tobin, Cullen, Joe O'Reilly, Batt O'Connor and Sinéad Mason knew of this war office address. His minister of finance offices were in Mary Street and Andrew Street. This man on the move never slept in any of his office-houses but always left his business premises complete with briefcase – a businessman.

Eventually he had up to thirty different hide-outs. One house which he used often was the 'second' home of Moya Llewelyn Davies. The beautiful, vivacious Moya, who had her main home in London, spent much of her time at her large house in Furry Park, Dublin, with its expanse of wooded land. Here, Mick could rely on Moya's confidentiality; she was sympathetic and discreetly supported Sinn Féin because of her own nationalist background. She fed Mick with 'an amount of information'; indeed she was one of his strong team of intelligence women. Often she had the inside track on the British cabinet 'meanderings', through her husband, according to Máire Comerford, a member of Cumann na mBan who had acted as an intermediary for Collins for the previous few years. The youthful breezy Máire could be seen any day darting through the streets of Dublin on her bicycle, a dispatch for Mick Collins tucked inside her bodice. When the information was too dangerous to be committed to paper, Máire would get word to Mick to meet Moya 'either at one of the many safe houses or in Furry Park'.

Moya, Mick, Máire and Liam Tobin had just finished having tea in a restaurant near the Pillar one day, when a group of Auxiliaries burst in. As they began to search, Mick slipped his gun on to Moya's lap. She stuffed it up the elastic leg of her knickers. Under his breath, Mick said, 'Follow me'. Over he went to the officer, held up his hands and, like a dutiful citizen, asked to be searched as they were in a hurry because the girls had a tram to catch. The officer searched the men and Mick took Moya's hand while Liam did the same with Máire. All four walked free into the night.[3]

The Keating branch of the Gaelic League at 46, Parnell Square continued to be a useful rendezvous for Mick and his associates, many of whom were members. Here Mick would meet intelligence officers, members of the Squad, other IRB men and members of Cumann na mBan. For an hour or two, serious business was conducted. Often Mick used the opportunity to give trusted people a warning dispatch to pass on to those he knew were on an arrest list.

One evening prior to a Gaelic League meeting Máire Comerford brought a document from Moya in code. Máire met Mick with Ned Broy and Kathleen Lynn, medical officer, at Devlin's – a bar where they often met. The four were walking down the street when Mick noticed a hold-up in the distance. 'Faint,' he whispered to Máire. She faked her faint and Mick held her. Between the three they sat her on the footpath. As the Auxiliaries approached Mick was fanning Máire's face with the secret document. While Ned Broy produced his Dublin Castle identification Mick said to Kathleen Lynn, 'Get your smelling salts!' Kathleen, who was loosening Máire's blouse, opened her medical bag, and soon Máire was 'revived', though she said, 'My heart was in my mouth. I could only think of what Mick held in his hand, but he was so calm.' Mick thanked the Auxiliary, who offered further help. Máire assured them she was fine again. She had been recovering from a dose of flu, Mick said. And so the four strolled off.[4]

One night Kathleen Napoli MacKenna arrived at Furry Park with an unexpected message, and discovered that Mick Collins was in the grounds searching for a 'tout' he had spotted. As the rain came down Mick let himself in the back door, while Kathleen stood under the elements at the hall door. He was not in a good mood.

Kathleen records that the tall, slim, graceful Moya was 'extremely elegant in a brown, gold-brocaded tight-fitting frock with long clinging sleeves, carefully-groomed ... a cigarette in a long holder between her slender tapering fingers' as she opened the door.[5]

It was this graceful demeanour that helped Moya through many tight corners and kept her above the suspicions of the authorities. The messages she gave Tommy Gay, the unassuming librarian, would be passed on promptly to Mick. Once a week, Mick would go on his old rusty bicycle to Gay's quiet suburban home in Clontarf to meet the G men who were his informants. In his head he would have decoded messages given to him by Moya or he would have carbon copies deciphered by his team of intelligence women. Or he would have data from letters intercepted by Dilly. His evenings could take him to meet Dilly from the mailboat and then to Howth or to Dalkey or other corners of the city. But here is a typical working day for Michael Collins at this time.

His first call in the early morning is to his intelligence office. He jots down points which have arisen overnight. When O'Reilly arrives with the papers he goes through them carefully, noting any political or military developments. Meanwhile, O'Reilly opens dispatches and letters, date-stamps them and pins them to the envelopes. Mick goes through them.

Sinéad Mason, his secretary and confidential typist, is almost his left hand. In the morning she assembles letters typed up the previous day and waits for his signature written in Irish and with ink, which sometimes comes with a smile. She makes suggestions regarding correspondence he has received and gives him some intelligence information. They agree on something that Ned Broy should be told. Mick jots down a note and sticks it inside his sock.

Sinéad is devoted to her work and loyal to Mick. He has total confidence in her. Despite great dangers she constantly undertakes nerve-racking tasks. Due to the peculiar circum-

66

stances of her work, ordinary office routine and hours are impossible. She has had to travel to various venues, transport important documents, according to Piaras Béaslaí, 'hither and thither, and meet Collins by appointment at different centres. His ceaseless energy [gives] her an immense amount of correspondence to deal with daily.'[6]

His business letters are exact, dictated now. It is the third quarter of 1920. A revolver rests at his elbow.

Despite his heavy workload and the risks involved Mick was always there for a friend in need. He found time to visit Batt O'Connor in hospital and made regular trips to Sinéad de Valera with fund-money to sustain her and her family while her husband, Éamon de Valera, was on the American fund-trail. When Dan Breen was shot in a Dublin raid and admitted to the Mater Hospital, he dropped in when he could. Friendly doctors and nurses colluded to keep the identities of the patient and visitor hidden.

Breen was recovering in Dr Alice Barry's house on the southside of Dublin when the block was surrounded by Auxiliaries. Though still with unhealed wounds, he made for the skylight but found he 'was caught like a rat in a trap,' as 'a solid line of khaki and steel lined up the street'. As usual a mass of spectators gathered. Breen surveyed them, and 'recognised the figure of Mick Collins'.

Mick, always ready to confront, had seen the troops moving in that direction and quickly 'collected a few of the boys who would be ready to attempt a rescue'. But it wasn't necessary, Dr Alice Barry's house was not among those raided.[7]

As raids and arrests increased, Brugha once more became absorbed in a plan for reprisals in England which went as far as proposing the bombing and gunning of civilian crowds in theatres and cinemas. He wanted to counter the wanton attacks on civilians in Ireland by the Black and Tans.

'You'll get none of my men for that,' Collins snapped.

'I want none of your men, Mr Collins,' said Brugha.

The cabinet rejected his plan totally. Brugha took this rebuff by Collins personally and pursued him with 'unrelenting hatred'. He was soon supported by Stack, who had once been Collins' friend and ally. This incident led to quarrels at cabinet meetings between Brugha and Stack and Collins. It also led to an anti-Collins faction outside the cabinet.[8]

By October 1920, with the spiralling of terror and counter-terror, life was becoming difficult in Ireland, and Lloyd George in a speech in Caernarvon talked of 'a murderous conspiracy' against his men.[9] But Mick was adamant that when 'an army of occupation terrorised a nation looking for its freedom ... our only way to carry on the fight is by organised and bold guerrilla warfare. But this in itself [is] not enough ... Without her Secret Service working at the top of its efficiency' England is helpless. 'It was these men we had to put out of the way,' he said.[10] Consequently, Mick went bald-headed for some secret service men who had been observing Dublin life since the middle of 1920. These men lived in private guesthouses throughout the city and masqueraded as businessmen. Because of their frequent visits to the Cairo Café, they were dubbed 'the Cairo gang' by Collins and his men. From the information given by women and men on the outside, and MacNamara, Broy, Neligan and Lily Mernin inside the Castle, Mick had a list of names. His agents in the sorting office intercepted the agents' mail and had it delivered to him. It was a battle of wits in the murky world of intelligence.

Many Dáil Éireann members and prominent Sinn Féin sympathisers had received threats written on the Dáil Éireann notepaper which had been lifted during the September raid on Sinn Féin headquarters. Mick was seriously alarmed by this development.

His intelligence system had penetrated the heart of the

British secret service. Memos of military communications were included in his documentation, and with Lily Mernin now well able to decipher carbon paper there were few British intelligence activities that evaded him. With his photographic memory, he could recall names, dates and documents. He became familiar with all the Castle personnel – military and civilians – their appearance, movements, habits and haunts. His initial source was the G men's leather-bound diaries held in the Castle office. Here the G men entered their day's activities, including suspects seen, where these went and the company they kept. Within the Castle walls Mick's men regularly read and copied G men's diaries for him.

By November 1920, he had evidence that the Cairo gang was becoming more and more dangerous. For some time he had the correspondence of these 'businessmen' scrutinised. Dilly and the women out in Howth were playing a pivotal role. With the aid of their landladies these men's wastepaper baskets were examined. Duplicate keys were made, also with the cooperation of landladies. Frank Thornton and a team of Collins' men kept a watching brief and logged the activities of each man. Then Frank Thornton was lifted, held and severely questioned, but was released after ten days. A raid on Vaughan's hotel had Liam Tobin and Tom Cullen jostled from their beds, held and closely questioned. They gave false names and managed to bluff their way out. Three nights later the hotel was again raided but Tobin and Cullen escaped through a window and spent some hours in an outhouse. And on 10 November, Richard Mulcahy escaped through the skylight in Professor Hayes' house at 5 am. 'We were being made to feel that they were very close on the heels of some of us,' Mulcahy remarked.[11]

It was around this time that Mick was in Amiens Street Station with Dilly Dicker one day; he was sending her on a mission. Suddenly they spotted the police. Mick leaped into one of the station's large luggage baskets, pulled the canvas covering over himself and told Dilly to hide him. In a flash, she was sitting on the basket and began to wave at an imaginary friend on the train.[12]

After all these close shaves, Mick could not fail to read the signs. Unless the Cairo gang was eliminated, the end was in sight for himself and many others. On 17 November he wrote to Dick McKee:

> Have established addresses of the particular ones. Arrangements should now be made about the matter. Lt. G is aware of things. He suggests the 21st, a most suitable date and day I think. M.[13]

The Lt. G. was 'a woman typist at army headquarters' who 'always signed her notes to him with the letter G'. The addition of Lt. was to create the impression that the agent was an army officer, should the letter be intercepted.[14]

There is no clue as to the identity of 'Lt. G'. Most of her notes gave information on troop movements, their strength and armaments, forthcoming activities of 'British Military Intelligence, the Auxiliaries and the Black and Tans'. There are, according to Rex Taylor, seventeen notes initialled by this 'G'.[15] Lt G. was in fact Lily Mernin.

Mick and his men were ready. He drew a detailed plan, setting out streets and routes, marked target houses and put Dick McKee and Peadar Clancy, commandant and vice-commandant Dublin brigade, in charge of the men chosen for house raids in different areas. At precisely 9 o'clock in the morning, on Sunday 21 November, eleven of the Cairo gang were shot dead in various locations, some in their beds in the presence of their wives or companions.

That day all hell broke loose. In the afternoon a Dublin-Tipperary football match was fixed for Croke Park. The match was in progress and the pitch densely packed with men, women and children when lorryloads of military invaded Croke Park and opened fire on the spectators and players.

There was panic and people tried to rush for cover. Thirteen spectators and a player, Michael Hogan, were killed, and a great number were wounded. 'Bloody Sunday', as it became known, made its mark on nationalist opinion.

In Dublin Castle, Dick McKee, the organiser of the assassination campaign, his associate Peadar Clancy and Conor Clune, an innocent football supporter picked up with McKee and Clancy, were tortured and killed. The official line was that they were shot 'while attempting to escape'.

Collins was among the congregation who attended Mass a few days later for the two men in the pro-cathedral. His wreath read: 'In memory of two good friends – Dick and Peadar – and two of Ireland's best soldiers. Mícheál Ó Coileáin. 25/11/20'.[16]

From this time on a reign of terror was instituted by the military forces. Curfew was proclaimed in Dublin from 10 pm. People were held up on the streets and searched. Outside Dublin the war intensified. The IRA flying columns and active service units grew. They arranged their own attacks on barracks and conducted ambushes, and for the most part worked independently of GHQ. They needed the support of local men, and especially of the women, who billeted them, gave them food, washed their clothes and attended to the wounded. These Volunteers took on the might of over 50,000 regular troops and 15,000 Black and Tans.

Because of widespread devastation an American Committee for Relief in Ireland had been established and food and clothes were sent in shiploads. To coordinate the materials and the money raised, the White Cross was established towards the end of 1920, with an executive which included women such as Hanna Sheehy Skeffington, Kathleen Clarke and Molly Childers. Máire Comerford and Leslie Price were recruited to travel to various counties for the White Cross and assembled information for Collins on the difficulties being experienced, particularly in the farming community by women who had to struggle with the work of the farm while husbands and sons were 'on the run'.[17]

The police had the impression of a reckless and flamboyant 'terrorist' and 'murderer' but Mick Collins maintained his businessman demeanour, seldom taking undue risks. When Harry Boland wrote a note from America cautioning Mick to be careful after so many arrests, Mick responded:

> I am in love with life as much as the next man. The escapes of others often chill me to the marrow. But for myself I take a logical view of things and act in accordance with what would seem to be a supersensitiveness.[18]

On 3 December the military found documents relating to G Division during a raid on the house of sympathiser Eileen McGrane. These were carbon copies given to Mick by Broy and stored in sacks by Eileen. Broy was immediately suspected. He was arrested and taken to Arbour Hill. Collins had Inspector Supple and Detective Inspector McCabe from the Castle intimidated into opening Broy's locker and box. They burned everything so that there was no evidence against Broy. To Collins' delight, Broy was released on bail, and the matter was never reactivated.

Meanwhile, down in Longford a decision had been taken by Seán MacEoin and the local brigade to eliminate RIC Inspector Kelleher, who had come to Longford, he said, 'to spill blood'. He lodged in the Greville Arms in Granard. On 31 October 1920, he was shot in the bar as he put down his half-finished glass of whiskey.

On the night of 3 November, eleven lorries of military entered Granard, sacked the town and burned down Kiernan's hotel. Larry Kiernan, Kitty and their three sisters were arrested. The others were held overnight but Kitty was detained for three days. Mick was upset. He remonstrated with MacEoin, saying that the hotel should not have been used as the place of execution.

72

Afterwards he wrote to Kitty, suggesting she come to Dublin for a chat. One night in late November 1920 Mick and Kitty talked well into the night in an upstairs room in Vaughan's Hotel, exchanging news of Harry Boland's activities.

The Kiernans, now homeless, stayed in Omard House, Granard. Later they would move to a large flat over a shop on the New Road.

Tentative peace moves were afoot in December 1920. Lloyd George wanted the Irish problem solved. He decided to make use of Griffith's arrest, knowing that Griffith was a moderate. Archbishop Clune of Perth, uncle of the murdered Conor Clune, arrived on the scene and was asked by influential people to see Lloyd George, who in turn suggested that he meet Arthur Griffith in prison. This he did. But he also met Mick Collins in Louise Gavan Duffy's school on St Stephen's Green. Mick was very conscious of security and left nothing to chance. Through warders in Mountjoy and through women visitors to the prison, Mick remained in close touch with Griffith but did not dare to visit him.

Collins was now in a difficult situation. He was acting president of Dáil Éireann since Griffith's arrest, as well as minister of finance. He was president of the IRB, director of intelligence, and director of munitions in the IRA Army Council and found it difficult to reconcile the military side with the first prospect of negotiations. In a letter published in the *Irish Independent* on 7 December he wrote: 'At the moment there is a very grave danger that the country may be stampeded on false promises and foolish ill-timed actions. We must stand up against that danger. My advice to the people is, "Hold fast"' and that: 'Everyone in Ireland has reason to be profoundly distrustful of British politicians of all schools ...'[19]

From experience Collins knew that Griffith was open to persuasion. He didn't want anybody to be under the illusion

73

that because Lloyd George could have direct access to Griffith he could solve the problem. 'Does anyone think that Mr Griffith will be so foolish as to negotiate with anybody from behind prison bars, away from his followers, and from his movement?' Collins wrote.[20]

On 23 December 1920 the Government of Ireland Act was passed. Ireland was to be divided against the will of the majority. On Christmas Eve morning 1920, with Collins' many agents aiding in the decoy, de Valera, dressed in clerical garb, arrived in Dublin. Mick and he had long discussions.

To celebrate Christmas, Mick that night dined in the Gresham Hotel in the company of Liam Tobin, Tom Cullen, Gearóid O'Sullivan and Rory O'Connor. They had dinner in the public dining-room, and had just finished when the waiter told them Auxiliaries were in the hall. They were on them immediately. All gave false names and addresses. Mick had the narrowest escape so far. He gave his name as John Grace, an accountant.

'Where do you work?' asked the officer.

'My office is in Dame Street,' said Collins.

In an ordnance survey map which he carried Mick had '6 Refills' scribbled in a corner – a reminder note. The officer tried to persuade him it was rifles. But his clear writing left no doubt, he said; it related to notebook refills which he used at work. The officer, distracted by trying to solve the question of the '6 Refills', didn't ask why he carried a map. Nevertheless, he was very suspicious. He took a photograph from his pocket and Collins kept up a pleasant smile as he eyed the revolver in the officer's pocket. He said afterwards that if he was going to be arrested, he would have snatched the revolver. 'The officer drew an old photograph of me out of his pocket and compared it with my face, drawing my hair down as it was in the picture,' he told Batt O'Connor afterwards. 'It was touch and go. They were not quite satisfied, and hesitated long before they left us,' he said.

The raiding party left and Collins got very drunk that night.[21]

WOMEN'S GUN-RUNNING ROLE

Mick was happy to see de Valera back home but soon after Christmas he had to fight off an attempt by de Valera, backed by Brugha and Stack, to send him to America to sort out some problems that had arisen in relation to fundraising. It made no sense to Collins for him to leave the country at this stage.

At a Dáil meeting Mick voiced his concern about the 'atrocities on women' such as the raid one night by men in mufti on the home of Agnes Daly in Limerick. She had a horrific experience, had her hand slashed and her hair cut with a razor, and gashes to her head. The Auxies used the excuse that she tried to run away from them, 'one young women against a group of strong men!'[1] Agnes, her sister Madge and Peg Barrett from Clare were on Collins' intelligence team. (The Daly girls were sisters of Kathleen Clarke, wife of executed 1916 leader Tom Clarke, and of Ned Daly, also killed in 1916; they were nieces of Fenian John Daly.) They were regular carriers of dispatches for Mick to and from the Limerick and Clare brigades, as were the Barrett sisters, Peg, Josephine and Dell.

The Daly girls helped in the running of the family bakery, and often travelled on the train with dispatches concealed in bags of flour. Mick would meet them at a bakery and flour shop off Parnell Square. One day Agnes, Madge and Peg Barrett were inside the bakery when the Auxies came on a raid. All three had important documents and Peg had proof that a spy going under the name of James Breen had been gathering information on Collins for some time. Breen, who masqueraded as a hat salesman, had become well known to Peg, who risked her life on many occasions to get information.

76

That day at the bakery door, a young man, 'cleaning' for a purpose, gave the signal with his whistling lilt. The three girls were 'sampling cakes' as they wished to place an order. Mick, dressed in a business suit, leaped over a bench at the first whistle, dipped his fingers in flour, ran them through his hair, and behind the bench leaned with pen poised. 'He was taking the girls' order,' Peg recalls, 'confidently telling them the difference between the texture of one cake and the other. I was a friend. That day we were about to smuggle guns down south.'

The raiders ripped open bags of flour, knocked over some trays of cakes, took plenty of buns and eventually departed, to the relief of all. The never-used oven with the false back held guns, as it had on other occasions. The girls brought some of these to Limerick and Clare in concealed pockets sewn on the shifts they wore underneath their long skirts.

'Breen' later met his death like other spies on Collins' track.[2]

Eileen McGrane, who kept important documents belonging to Collins, was in her flat one evening when it was raided. Not alone did the raiders carry away important documents but she was arrested and courtmartialled – the first courtmartial of a woman. She did not betray any secrets. She was kept in custody for many months. Other women had the same fate. Mick was enraged, also because 'the enemy took a whole lot of my old private letters – poor mother's mortuary card not being left even,' he told his sister, Helena (Sr Celestine): 'Surely there must have been some one of yours [letters] among them. They raided all the known addresses ... I wonder if you were raided!'[3]

By now areas in Dublin were being 'combed out', the inhabitants harassed and searched. Citizens of Dublin had grown to accept the abnormal conditions. The campaign against the crown forces intensified. Collins constantly varied his tactics, and if he suspected a person was curious, he 'invented Gyntian romances'. Often he pretended to others that he had a date with a girl.[4] So compartmentalised were his intelligence activities that when he was going out to Dalkey or Howth with Dilly he would get rid of 'those in 44' by saying that they had been invited to a house party.[5] A common ploy used by Mick as well as by others in his intelligence department was to walk down the street linked to a likely young girl.

There were moments of light relief. During the difficult days of January 1921, Mick was a guest at a party given by an Irish-American attorney, James M. Sullivan, at his home in Palmerston Park. Most of the guests were 'wanted', but among them were three G men – Broy, MacNamara and Neligan. The host was unaware of their identity. Many of Collins' intelligence women were there also – Moya Llewelyn Davies, Máire Comerford, Brigid Lyons-Thornton, Jennie Wyse-Power.

Mick had already imported arms, mainly from Glasgow and Liverpool, and had also been involved in the importation of arms from Italy through his friend Dónal Hales. There were dispatches and pleas to him, especially from the three Cork brigades, that they were in urgent need of arms as they were 'harassed to a terrible extent by the enemy'.

Dónal's sister, Madge, had already been to Italy in December 1920 and by March 1921 was about to embark on another trip. She was a key link in the arms importation and carried many of Mick's instructions in her head. Often her brother would write to her and she would travel to Dublin by train from Cork to convey the message to Mick. She was also in a position to decode some of Dónal's ambiguous statements in his letters to Collins. Madge was the link between Collins and Liam Deasy and his Third West Cork Brigade, members of which were involved in preparing dumps for the arms.[6]

Liam Mellows became director of purchases, in charge of the importation of arms. IRA money had for some time been channelled through the IRB for the arms purchases. Cathal Brugha, who had a deep dislike and distrust of the IRB, used the discrepancies in the transfer of money as a tactic to fault Collins. Collins had been administering two sources of revenue – the public money voted by Dáil Éireann and the secret funds of the IRA and IRB. Though he tried to separate them, often they overlapped. Money was always on the go. A sailor on his way to Hamburg was given money to bring back revolvers but he might not return. Money was given to men unaccustomed to bookkeeping on the off-chance of a substantial purchase. Sentries had to be 'squared', so too had loading men and taxi-drivers.

One night, quantities of Mick's papers had been seized in a raid on a house in Bachelor's Walk. These included expense accounts for arms purchased in England and their loss made Mick's task of accounting more difficult. Brugha continued to nag for better accounting and was aided by Austin Stack and Liam Mellows. The entire affair upset Collins. 'Cathal is jealous of Mick,' Richard Mulcahy said.[7]

Beaten on this front, Brugha returned 'to his old mania' – his plan to assassinate the British cabinet. He knew Mick's dislike of this policy, so unknown to him he summoned some daring Volunteers to Dublin. He made Seán MacEoin leader of this London operation. Brugha would not listen to MacEoin's objections. MacEoin then went to Mulcahy, who sent him to Collins. 'You should be at home attending to your business,' was Collins' response. 'Do you think that England has the makings of only one cabinet?' On his way back to Mullingar MacEoin was shot by British forces, wounded and arrested. That evening, Mick attempted but failed to rescue him. Later MacEoin was sentenced to death.

On 12 February 1921, Mick who had been in constant touch with Leslie Price, sometimes through her brother Mick Price, sent her a note:

Dearest Leslie
Try to meet me at the usual place on Thursday, 8.30 p.m.
Love, M.

The 'usual place' was Moya Llewelyn Davies' house at Furry Park. At other times he would use 'J's place' – that was Jennie Wyse-Power's house. Mick always used Dearest Leslie, Leslie Dearest or some such endearment. He did the same to Moya and the rest and this made the note look like a love note if it was intercepted. 'If he had important information in a dispatch, this would be in code, we would decipher it [the dispatch] and then destroy ... because the code could be captured. These [codes] were constantly being changed,' according to Leslie.

That evening, 12 February, Leslie went to Moya's house. She had returned from west Cork a few days previously and had told Mick that Tom Barry was pleading for guns. Over a number of months Leslie had been travelling throughout Cork by bicycle or pony and trap, organising Cumann na mBan. Periodically she would return to Mick at GHQ with Cork brigade details. She had occasionally taken one or two guns in her handbag or luggage. But now she was on a bigger mission.

Moya had a motor car. Moya and Leslie prepared for the journey in Moya's house. In bags of flour they hid the wrapped guns. Mick told them 'to dress up'. Leslie was nervous because the previous year (1920) Linda Kearns had been arrested and sentenced to ten years for driving a car full of arms. (With the aid of a friendly warder and local Volunteers, Linda and her comrades Eithne Coyle, Aileen Keogh and Mary Burke escaped from Mountjoy Jail by means of a rope ladder.)

Moya, 'dressed as a real lady with flamboyant hat' and Leslie, clad likewise, set out for Cork early next morning. They were stopped at several places, but 'Moya was very capable'. Most of the guns were left at O'Mahony's of Belrose near Upton and used later by Tom Barry's flying column.

On 24 February Leslie got another, 'Dearest Leslie' note from Mick. This time Moya and she had a smaller quantity of guns for Liam Lynch. These were again carefully packed by 'a few of the girls' and next morning, with Mick's blessing, the two 'ladies' set out for Mourne Abbey outside Mallow for the Cork Number Two Brigade. They had a narrow escape beyond Cashel when they almost ran into an ambush.

Their next journey came after a 'My Dearest Leslie' note from Mick on 2 March 'for the usual place'. This mission would take Moya and Leslie to Cork Number One Brigade. They had a small consignment which they wrapped in underwear, 'corsets and camisoles', with other clothes, and hid in cases. They got a puncture not far from Dublin and a lorryload of Auxiliaries stopped when they saw 'the ladies in distress'. They were happy to change the wheel and send them on their way. Nora O'Leary and Lil Conlon later took Moya, Leslie and their 'precious load' to a house on the outskirts of Douglas.[8]

On another mission some time previously, Nancy O'Brien was returning from England with a case containing guns for Mick. She got off the tram and was obviously having difficulty lifting the load. A policeman kindly offered to help her, and she 'gladly' agreed. Mick said, 'That's one way of bringing in guns!'[9]

In early 1921, the hunt for Mick Collins continued. He was at dinner in Linda Kearns' nurses' home one day when suddenly Auxiliaries burst in. Mick, plate and cutlery in hand, in a split second slid under the table. Shielded by the diners and the tablecloth he crouched while the Auxies breezed past to look under beds, in cupboards, and corners. Mick and plate did not emerge until the last sound of the military had died and Linda gave the all-clear.

One night during a raid in Donnybrook, the officer in charge stumbled on some love-letters and became engrossed.

The young woman who owned the letters chastised him for invading her privacy. While hastily trying to stuff them into the drawer the officer also pushed in his list of houses to be raided. Next day Mick learned of his narrow escape. Sinéad Mason's house, where he had slept the previous night, was on the list.

Mick's reputation for elusiveness grew. A report in the *Daily Sketch* claimed that he led an ambush in Burgatia near his west Cork birthplace on a white horse: '20 constables were attacked by 400 rebels ...' – a greatly exaggerated account of Tom Barry and his flying column. The incident amused Mick.

In a letter on 5 March to his sister Helena (Sister Celestine) he noted:

> The English papers have been giving me plenty of notoriety – a notoriety one would gladly be rid of but they must make a scapegoat. *Daily Sketch* had a gorgeous thing once upon a time – 'Mike' the super hater, dour, hard, no ray of humour, no trace of human feeling – oh lovely! The white horse story was an exaggeration. I have not ridden a white horse since I rode 'Gipsy' and used her mane as a bridle.[10]

Broy again came under suspicion by Dublin Castle and was arrested. His superintendent had no knowledge of his dual role but trusted him and so thought it wise to burn all papers in his policeman's locker. The Castle authorities were unable to sustain any charge against him but they kept him in Arbour Hill. Mick was devastated but this time it was impossible to plan an escape as life in the city was getting too hot. Broy remained in custody until after the Truce.

Shortly after this MacNamara came under suspicion, was dismissed, and ordered to get out of the Castle instantly and never return. 'You're lucky,' was Mick's response. 'If they had any suspicion of the real state of affairs, your life wouldn't be spared.'

MacNamara now began work with Collins' own intelligence staff. Neligan, who had been sworn into the secret service, remained undetected. The day after his 'swearing in' he took a copy of his oath to Collins. 'To the ends of the earth' they would follow him if he betrayed the service! 'But betray it I did. For Ireland and for Mick Collins!'[11]

Raids, Arrests,
Suspicion of Betrayal

January 1921 brought sad personal news for Mick. Kathy, wife of his brother Johnny (and sister of Mick's friend Seán Hurley who was killed in 1916), had died. He tried to go to the funeral, but a hold-up at the railway station meant he had to duck so he missed the train.

Afterwards he wrote to his sister Helena:

> Poor Kathy is gone, alas! She is a loss not only to Johnny and all them splendid children but to the locality generally. She was a splendid type of Irish mother and many a person in South Cork will mourn her loss.[1]

He tried to keep contact with his family but it wasn't always easy. Not having been in touch with his sister Mary in Cork for a few weeks, he wrote: 'You know it is through no lack of feeling nor indeed through any lack of thought for you but those to whom I write are doomed to have trouble brought upon them'. He wondered if she had been raided. 'As one of the great English officers said recently on a raid – "Anyone who is a friend of that man is bound to suffer".'[2]

In early April, Mick's intelligence office in Mespil Road was raided. In a desk beside the window the raiders found a brace of loaded revolvers. Fortunately, Mick's intelligence files were hidden in one of Batt O'Connor's secret cupboards. When the British had completed their search they occupied the building, hid all signs of their presence and prepared to sit until Mick rode up in the morning, pushed his bike around the side and strode in the door.

They had already arrested Patricia Hoey, who with her invalid mother occupied the upstairs portion of the house. Aware of the danger for Mick Collins she bluffed her way, saying she was a journalist and that the press of the world would hear the story of their treatment of a woman. Late into the night she pleaded with them to let her go back to her mother. Eventually they agreed. Though under guard, she managed to tell her mother to fake a collapse. After further discussion they allowed her out under escort to fetch a doctor. Her mother couldn't be examined with men present, she told them, and they agreed to withdraw. Patricia then told the doctor her predicament.

Further consternation. No one knew where Mick was staying. Through the network, they succeeded with Joe O'Reilly's help in getting scouts posted at every road leading to the office. And so, that bright spring morning, Collins, Cullen and Alice Lyons, the secretary, were all halted in time. It was a devastating blow because Mick now knew the military had the inside track, that they had been acting on a tip-off. The office would have to be abandoned.

His dear friend and intelligence agent, Moya Llewelyn Davies, was arrested when her home was raided one night. She was lucky that no guns were found on the premises. She was imprisoned and her husband Crompton was dismissed from his British government post.[3]

Moya's arrest and those of Eileen McGrane and Patricia Hoey upset Mick. He disliked the thought of women being confined to what he termed 'dismal surroundings'. He got his warder contacts in Mountjoy to see that they received 'little comforts' such as woollen rugs, good books, and food. He knew Moya liked China tea so he had it smuggled in to her with sweetmeats and 'other goodies' for all three.[4]

At the time Mick was planning Seán MacEoin's escape using the help of Dr Brigid Lyons. On many occasions the vibrant, energetic Brigid had transported revolvers, ammunition as well as dispatches for MacEoin and his brigade members in Longford. In this intriguing and nerve-wracking work, while still continuing her medical duties, she often only escaped arrest by the tips of her fingers. Now she would be a key link between Collins and MacEoin who was in George V Military Hospital, having been wounded while trying to escape arrest. She succeed in getting parcels and secret notes to MacEoin but was not allowed see him. MacEoin's planned escape by Collins was foiled when he was suddenly transferred to Mountjoy Jail. Using her charm Brigid got the authorities in Mountjoy to believe that she was involved in a romantic relationship with MacEoin, and was granted visitation permits to his military hospital bed. This allowed Collins to plan another escape.

Using every trick, Brigid and Seán MacEoin discreetly exchanged 'intimate' notes and coded messages during visits. Despite a clamp down on one occasion when MacEoin's friend and fellow prisoner Thomas Traynor was court-martialled then hanged on 26 April, Brigid, on Collins' advice, succeeded in getting her permits renewed. (Questioning by Castle authorities for each permit was rigorous.) There were several hitches in this escape plan as MacEoin, who faced court-martial was moved from the hospital area to another part of the prison.

Throughout this time Collins, Emmet Dalton and some Squad members were planning the rescue of MacEoin, while Brigid used her charm as a go-between. Due to a series of events on the day of the planned rescue MacEoin was unable to be in the governor's office at the time Emmet Dalton, Tom Keogh and Joe Leonard, dressed in captured British military uniforms, had entered. Shots were exchanged and the men were lucky to escape the machine-gun fire. It was with a heavy heart Brigid, who was attached to Hollis Street hospital at the time, learned of the foiled attempt. However, with Collins' encouragement she continued her visits to Mountjoy, while Collins began planning another rescue. He visited Mrs MacEoin in Longford. 'Next time I come, I'll bring him with me, and it won't be long either,' he told her. While in Longford he paid a brief visit to Kitty Kiernan,

Harry Boland's girlfriend, with whom he could freely discuss confidential matters.

A few weeks later Brigid informed Collins that the date of Seán's court-martial was eminent. During the trial, which took place in June 1921, he was found guilty and sentenced to death for the murder of a member of the crown forces. (A short time later when the truce was being discussed MacEoin was still in custody. In one of the terms for further discussion with Lloyd George, de Valera insisted on MacEoin's release and so forced Lloyd George to relent.)

Meanwhile Mick was heartened by the success of the guerrilla campaign in his native west Cork. On 19 March, Tom Barry and his flying column had successfully out-fought lorryloads of Tans and Auxiliaries at Crossbarry. This success brought new hope to the IRA throughout Ireland, and was followed by another successful ambush at Rosscarbery Barracks.

Mick Collins was so elated at the capture of his home barracks that he wrote on 7 April about 'the splendid performance' and expressed a wish to meet Tom Barry, 'the officer who arranged this encounter and carried it out with such gallantry and efficiency'.[5]

But his elation was short-lived. Just over a week later, 16 April, in revenge for the Rosscarbery ambush, the dreaded Essex Regiment under Major Percival burned houses in the area including the Collins family home. His brother Johnny, who was in Cork at a county council meeting, was captured as he got off the train in Clonakilty, informed that his home had been burned, taken to Cork Prison and thence to Spike Island.

News that the Auxiliaries had rounded up neighbours and as hostages got them to pile hay inside the house and sprinkle it with petrol before setting it alight upset Collins greatly. 'They know how to hurt me most,' he said, 'and those splendid children, already without a mother and now without a father or a home.'[6] He worried about the treatment Johnny would receive, being his brother.

He was to remember this event and recall it on the last day of his life when he returned to his old home.[7]

Though de Valera was pressing for negotiations to open up again with Lloyd George, Collins was determined to fight 'until we win'. Aware of the problem in the 'north-east' since the Government of Ireland Act of 1920, he was determined that the end result should be 'an Irish republic'.[8]

In mid-May 1921, Tom Barry, 'a wanted man', posed as a medical student to travel by train to Dublin. In Devlin's pub he met Gearóid O'Sullivan and for the first time he met Mick – the man who had praised him for the Rosscarbery ambush. The day after Barry left Dublin (he had also met de Valera during this visit) the Customs House – centre of nine departments of British administration – was destroyed. The next day Mick had the closest shave of his career. With Gearóid O'Sullivan, he lunched in Woolworth's as he had often done. The young girl who served them was extremely attentive, and for some reason Mick had a hunch.

'We'll have to stop coming here,' he said. 'She has us taped.' Rather than returning immediately to his Mary Street office, he suggested to O'Sullivan that they go for a drink. He then told O'Sullivan that he'd go on to his office. 'I've a feeling there's something wrong in Mary Street,' he said.

Back in Mary Street, Ellie Lyons, Mick's typist, remarked to Sinéad Mason that Mick was over half an hour late. Just as the two spoke they were startled by a noise. A few Auxiliaries dashed up the stairs past Ellie as she walked across the landing. One Auxie, on finding the back room locked, demanded the key from her. 'We know Collins is in there!' he shouted. Then hearing what sounded like a scuffle on the landing above, he moved to look. In that few seconds she and Sinéad tripped down the stairs and past the sentries before the alarm sounded.

88

This was the second raid on this office within a few weeks. Joe O'Reilly had escaped through the skylight and set out to find Mick. For the first time he found him 'rattled ... deathly pale and agitated' at the news. Later that evening when Mick visited O'Connor's, Mrs O'Connor got the same impression. And that night in Devlin's he broke down.

'There's a traitor in the camp,' he repeated. He told Batt O'Connor that he felt the game was up for him.[9]

Mick moved office again, this time to St Andrew's Street. The military were close on his heels. Less than a week later, in a letter to de Valera, he said that 'the escape on Thursday was nothing to four or five escapes I have had since. They ran me very close for quite a good while on Sunday evening.'[10]

Raids on houses which he frequented made him uneasy and he had a strong suspicion of betrayal by someone he knew. On 9 June, in a letter which was smuggled in to Moya Llewelyn Davies in jail, he wrote, 'The chase I think has not been less hot. They have got several items of information. They got them by torture and extraction'.[11] Yet he was adamant that mentally he was not on the run, as he told Moya two weeks later:

> I have (or think I have) a fair knowledge of the mental attitude of the others, and he is on the run who feels he is on the run. I have avoided that feeling. Others have not – it is these who make themselves remarkable by their actions and movements.[12]

It appears that shortly after this Collins found out who the informer was and had him shot.

Throughout May the British cabinet had been discussing ways of getting the Irish leaders to talk peace but Mick's priority was action. He was in regular correspondence with the commanding officer and intelligence officer of every working brigade. Despite IRA losses and difficulties, they continued countrywide operations throughout May and June.

However, Collins and GHQ were unable to supply arms in response to the pleas of the three Cork brigades. Mick sent Madge Hales to her brother in Italy to try to speed up the shipment of arms that was expected.[13]

Madge Hales arrived back from Italy in June and informed Mick that only half a boatload of armaments could be obtained; this, coupled with transport difficulties, meant that the anticipated shipment had been postponed once again.[14] The serious shortage of arms hampered the fight, 'because men, no matter how determined they may be, or how courageous, cannot fight with their bare hands'.[15] Collins neglected to inform the Cork brigades of the failure of the Italian shipment because he had so much on his mind; this was held against him at a time of future division.

Soon Lloyd George invited de Valera to come to London for discussions. De Valera took with him Erskine Childers and a delegation of four cabinet colleagues, including Austin Stack. Collins was anxious to go but Dev 'flatly refused to have him, and there were some bitter words between them'.[16] Arising out of the negotiations it was obvious to de Valera that ultimately 'some form of partition would be a part of any settlement.[17] These talks as well as other pressures on the British government led to the Truce.

Monday, 11 July 1921 was a sunny day. Before noon armoured tanks, cars and patrols made a slow procession back to barracks. Then at noon church bells and clocks struck. Truce time. The public was happy that the guns were silent but for Collins and his comrades there was the danger that once they came out into the open, they would be easily 'exterminated' if the Truce should fail.

In Harcourt Terrace, Mick Collins sat at his desk, retrieved slips of paper from his socks and began to write.

TRUCE, INTRIGUE, TREATY NEGOTIATIONS

Two days after the Truce began Mick Collins was again at his desk in Harcourt Street. He had come to realise that there were many divisions within the ranks of the IRA and Sinn Féin, as well as jealousy and clashes of personality. It hurt him deeply that Cathal Brugha, Austin Stack and Liam Mellows often undermined his ideas and comments but he was more hurt that de Valera did not see things in the same light as he did.

Although the Truce was in force, Mick decided that he should continue planning in case of the resumption of hostilities. He went to country brigades, spoke to commands, inspected training camps, set out to reorganise his intelligence system, and continued gun-running.

In the early days of the truce, he wished to preserve his anonymity. He was one of the party in the Mansion House at which 'celebrities' were present. When de Valera left 'he was cheered again & again', Mick told his friend, Moya. He said he made a bet that he'd go out unrecognised.

> Out I goes and not a look or token of recognition. I was awfully pleased – just to know I was right & there were dozens there who knew me & would have gone mad over it but I was down the steps & through the crowd with Messenger Boy rapidity.[1]

Soon his thoughts turned to home. He would visit Woodfield, meet the neighbours and if possible see his brother Johnny, still a prisoner on Spike Island. On a fine July day he took the train from Dublin to Clonakilty. He made no effort at disguise, and believed that not 'a single one of their agents laid eyes knowingly' on him. 'That was my intention and I think I carried it out successfully,' he wrote to Moya.

Despite being unable to get a permit to see Johnny, he said he was very glad to have gone on the two-day trip to Cork.[2]

He told de Valera: 'the spirit animating the enemy in Cork city and in the parts of the county I visited is arrogant and provocative. They are trying to regard the position not as a truce but as a surrender on our part'.[3]

When Seán MacEoin wasn't released with the other prisoners on 6 August, Collins protested: 'No discussions without MacEoin!' He was promptly released.

Mick knew, as did all the other military men and women, that activity was essential for those who had been on permanent active service for some time, that a period of prolonged uncertainty could make the man with the gun a law unto himself. While de Valera talked, the country began to drift towards anarchy. It was essential that negotiations should be rapidly pushed to a conclusion. He said to Moya that 'the days ahead are going to be the truly trying ones and we can only face them with set faces and hearts full of hope and confidence. It would be very dreadful if we did anything wrong'.[4]

Although intelligence work continued, and Dáil and cabinet matters absorbed much of his time, Mick had more room in his life for pleasure during the early days of the Truce. He asked the Leigh Doyles to take himself and Harry Boland in their recently purchased car to the Devil's Glen in Rathdrum. Here he met other comrades and on that sunny July day they all sat down to a memorable picnic. It was as if he did not want the day to end. He played with children, stumbled on one occasion and fell into the shallow water.

He also had the opportunity to go Granard more often and more openly to visit the Kiernans. In mid-July he went to Granard with Harry Boland where they met all the Kiernan sisters but spent time especially with Kitty. The slim, five foot five Kitty was lively, good-looking, practical and liked the good things in life. Before the military came to burn down their home in November, all had a quick chance to take something, and while Maud took the account book, Chrys the religious objects, Helen the dresses, Kitty took the silver.

While Harry Boland was engaged in conveying messages between de Valera and Lloyd George, Mick paid another visit to Granard on his own. During a long walk in the garden Mick sensed warmth from Kitty and asked her to come with him to the Horse Show in Ballsbridge. By this time, he had no special girlfriend, although he had many female friends. He was still friendly with Susan Killeen and Dilly Dicker, who continued to work with him.

On 2 August Mick dropped a line to Kitty. Checking his calendar he discovered that the Horse Show was a week away. 'That's a very long time to wait to see you. At the moment I don't know if I'll be able to go down for the coming weekend, but I'll try ... When do you come up yourself? ... Am really anxious to see you,' he wrote.[5]

The Horse Show of 1921 was a great occasion. Mick, Kitty, Harry, Richard Mulcahy, Celia Gallagher and a number of other friends met up there.

A few days later Harry was once more on a mission for de Valera, but on 21 August Mick wrote to Kitty: 'Harry is back here this morning. Will that entice you to come to town, to give you that chance to which he is entitled? Do you remember what I said about this?' She had obviously given Mick grounds for some hope, but because of his friendship with Harry, he wanted her to make her own decision.[6]

It was too late to post this letter and besides he had no stamps. On the following day he got a letter of rebuke from Kitty. So to 'avoid a misunderstanding' he wrote immediately 'under great difficulties at a Dáil meeting' because he wondered if she was angry with him 'because I did not travel [to Granard] yesterday but I had to work.'[7]

On 31 August he wondered how she was 'now – and since'. His arrangements the previous night 'were shattered' because he had 'to talk very very high politics from 10.30 to 2.30', in Wicklow. And the night before that he had been meeting the IRB in order to defend Harry's stance in the US conflict between de Valera and the Clan na Gael leaders. Defending Harry – 'Isn't that rather nice?' he asked Kitty.[8]

In fact he did not give Kitty the full story of his extremely busy schedule but he wrote from Wicklow to Moya Llewelyn Davies:

> I was up at 5 am Sunday morning and the next time I took off my clothes was at 4.30 am on Tuesday morning ... I was on the road again at 7.30 that morning. This will show you what the peaceful restfulness of the Truce is.[9]

A general election had been held in May to give effect to the Government of Ireland Act, which had been passed to establish separate parliaments in northern and southern Ireland. Collins had been returned for Armagh as well as Cork.

Now the Dáil asked him to go to Armagh. 'I must do it although I hate a public meeting like I hate a plague ... I'm going to endeavour making such an appeal to them as will make them rock to their foundations – at least I'm going to try,' he told Moya.[10]

Very early on Sunday morning Mick, with his secretary, Sinéad Mason, Harry Boland, Vinny Byrne and Joe Hyland, headed for Armagh, where, Harry Boland said in a letter to Kitty, they 'had a very strenuous day.'[11]

When the youthful Mick with the dark moustache leaped up, threw himself over the platform rail and stretched out his hands there was an instant storm of cheering. He appealed to the Orangemen 'to join with us, as Irishmen to come into the Irish nation ... to come in and take their share in the government of their own country'.[12]

Back in Dublin, he wrote to Kitty next day; he told her about his busy schedule which included a visit to 'the head of Blessed Oliver Plunkett' in Drogheda where he lit a candle for her.[13]

Two days later Harry Boland wrote to Kitty, saying he

expected to be in Scotland later in the month as talks of negotiations were on the horizon; he 'very much' wished to see her before taking the trip. However, as she was on holidays in Donegal, he would 'wait patiently for a later day' if needs be. 'If you see a wee bit of white heather, you might pluck it for me and send it for luck on my Scotch trip.'[14]

Harry travelled to Granard to be with Kitty on 18 September, but felt he had to return too soon. Meanwhile, Collins and Gearóid O'Sullivan sent telegrams to him to Granard, but he had left before these arrived. He would like to 'double-cross' the pair, he wrote to Kitty afterwards. 'It seems to me that I have a hard road to travel ere I can call you my very own!'[15]

That night Harry had met up with 'the bunch' and went with them to a show in the Gaiety and to supper in the Gresham. He told her, 'many of my pals (?) asked "How did you (meaning me) get on at Granard?" To all of which I failed to respond'. By now their comrades knew that he and Mick were rivals for Kitty's heart. He wrote this letter to her before going to bed. He wanted to tell her how much he had enjoyed the trip and 'to say how lonely I feel to-night. Even during the gayest moments of the evening I was all the time thinking of you, *sweetheart*, and am certain you and I will be for all time lovers'. He finished the letter, 'Goodnight, sweet love, and I am certain I will win you against the formidable opponent with which I am faced. God bless and guard you until we meet again. Sweetheart, good night. XXX, XXXXX'.[16]

Meanwhile, on the political scene, letters were exchanged between de Valera and the British government which led ultimately to the appointment of five plenipotentiaries to a conference in London.

De Valera, who would not lead the delegation, insisted, 'from the personal touch and contact I had with the mind of the Minister of Finance [Michael Collins] that I felt I knew that he was absolutely vital to the delegation'. Collins protested 'with all the vehemence at his command'. He believed that because of his extreme reputation his name could be better used at home. During the previous negotiations Collins had asked to go to London with de Valera, but now that Britain was rejecting the Republican claim he felt he was being used merely as a scapegoat by some Dáil members.

After a heated debate he addressed the Dáil: 'To me the task is a loathsome one. If I go, I go in the spirit of a soldier who acts against his judgement at the orders of a superior officer'.[17]

That evening he was morose. He went to Batt O'Connor's house. Batt said:

> I will never forget his agony of mind. He would not sit down, but kept pacing up and down the floor, saying that he should not be put in that position; that it was an unheard of thing that the soldier who had fought the enemy in the field should be selected to carry on negotiations. He said it was de Valera's job, not his.[18]

He was agitated and could not sleep. 'I remained out of bed last night until four this morning,' he told Kitty, in whom he had sensed a coolness. 'If you are still keeping up that hideous resolution of yours about not writing, I suppose I shall hear from you when I see you and not until then. Is it so, love?'[19]

Collins was to be second-in-command of the five man delegation. Griffith would be chairman, Robert Barton, economic expert; Éamonn Duggan and George Gavan Duffy lawyers, Erskine Childers and John Chartres secretaries, and Fionán Lynch and Diarmuid O'Hegarty assistant secretaries.

The credentials stated that the delegates were 'Envoys Plenipotentiary from the elected Government of the Republic in Ireland to negotiate and conclude with the representatives of His Britannic Majesty George V a Treaty or Treaties of association and accommodation between Ireland and the

Community of Nations known as the British Commonwealth.' In a further directive the cabinet gave them instructions under which 'the complete text of the draft Treaty' about to be signed was to be 'submitted to Dublin and reply awaited.'[20]

The delegates were in a paradoxical position, which has been a source of endless debate and discussion. They were to take with them de Valera's draft document of 'External Association'.[21] Though the delegates had only 'a hazy conception of what it would be in its final form,' according to Barton, 'What was clear was that it meant that no vestige of British authority would remain in Ireland'.[22]

Mick had sworn allegiance to the Republic, but he knew now that the national aspirations might have to be compromised. He decided he would go to Cork to preside at a divisional meeting of the IRB which was held at Nora O'Brien's house in Parnell Place. Though those present were IRB officers, the integration with the IRA in the south was so complete that the two organisations were in agreement on methods and objectives.

Prior to the meeting Collins told Liam Lynch and some other officers that 'some modifications of the full Republican demand might have to be made in the London negotiations, if a settlement was to be reached'. However, he did not mention this when speaking at the meeting, but said they had earned 'the right to be consulted before any final decision was reached on whatever terms of settlement were proposed by the British, and that for his part he would do his best to see that they were consulted'. Whether it was due to an oversight, or pressure of work, the Cork activists did not receive any further communication until 12 December, after the Treaty had been signed.[23]

LOVE TRIANGLE

De Valera now instructed Harry Boland to go to America, and like a good soldier he obeyed. He had asked Kitty to follow him and marry him there. Down in Cork on 1 October, preparing for his trip across the Atlantic, he was feeling 'just lonely and sad as the day itself, and God knows this is a real Cork day, raining soft and persistent!' he wrote to Kitty.

'I'm wondering if you are ever a wee bit lonely for me; and are you longing as I am for the day when we shall meet again? R.S.V.P.' Harry didn't know if he was making a mistake in leaving Kitty behind. He asked her to send a cable to the liner *The Celtic* just saying *Yes* 'and if you are still in doubt, then for God's sake try to make up your mind, and agree to come with me,' he pleaded.[1]

Mick and he had spent the previous night chatting over a few drinks. Both were going away. They hoped the conference would bring peace, although they both feared war.

Mick saw Harry to his home at 2 am on the night prior to Harry's departure for New York. 'And as I had to catch the 7.35 am I bade him goodbye,' Harry wrote to Kitty, 'only to find him at Kingsbridge as fresh as a daisy to see me off. I need not say to you how much I love him, and I know he has a warm spot in his heart for me, and I feel sure no matter what manner our triangle may work out, he and I shall be always friends.'

'All the time I shall carry you with me in my heart,' he told her, and pleaded for a photo, 'one that I can carry in my match or cigarette case. Have a good chat with Father Shanley, and do come back with him and marry me, after which we shall go to California for our honeymoon ... I bid you a fond farewell and, as I can not kiss you with my lips, I do so a million times with the lips of my heart.' And he ended with, 'Your devoted lover, Harry.'[2]

Next day he sent her a farewell note from Cobh before

departure. He wished her 'a very happy and pleasant time in Dublin next week'. Though knowing she would be meeting Mick, Harry begged her: 'Write to me often and I shall be happy ... May God guard you and direct you. Say a wee prayer now and then for your wandering lover – Love without end. Harry'.[3]

As he set sail on 3 October, he sent her a 'Goodbye, love' telegram, then another as he passed Kerry and one from New York announcing that he had 'arrived safe and well' on 11 October.

Harry's mother wrote to Kitty:

> As Harry tells me you are engaged to be married to him, allow me to congratulate you ... a better son never lived than Harry ... you know the old saying 'a good son makes a good husband' ... I hope to meet you next time you are in town.[4]

Harry wrote to Kitty every day while crossing the Atlantic and on 14 October he asked her not to tell his colleagues of his 'great hope' that they would be married in America. Though they were unofficially engaged, Harry was still uncertain of her love because of her fondness for Mick.

Kitty was staying in Dublin with her sisters. Mick sent her a note asking her to come with him to the Shelbourne Park fête – a prisoners' fundraising event. 'I want no one else but just yourself. If you can come I'll be at the Gresham at 8. If you can't come, I shall understand.'[5]

Kitty went with him to the fête and afterwards she dropped him a note which 'was a delight' to him. 'Am working almost asleep,' he wrote on the night before his departure for London. 'Can't write any more. Am thinking of you, and in a nice nice way. Eyes are closed, or almost.'[6]

The next day he wrote a seven-page letter on Gresham Hotel notepaper and another page from his notebook to 'My dear dear Kit'. It was to be his 'last act' before going to London for the negotiations. 'Goodness knows I have a heavy heart this moment, but there is work to be done and

I must not complain. The memory of the last few meetings – whatever comes – will be a pleasure and comfort to me ... I feel today that arrangements of ours may be made more binding – do you think so?' He wondered if she had thought over the preliminary proposal which he had made.

He was glad she liked the present of a writing set which he gave her. They had made a pact that they would write to each other every few days and with a writing set she had no excuse: 'If I write you to come to London you will, won't you? ... One thing ... finally ... those few charming hours have placed on me while in London a restraint which I probably would not otherwise have felt. That is a good thing for me, and may be a good thing for our mission'.[7] He had hopes now of winning her.

That Sunday night, 9 October, he crossed to London, and on the Monday morning newspaper there was a story that Collins himself boasted that he got to London unnoticed. He wrote to Kitty, 'I never said such a thing, Newspapermen are inventions of the devil'.[8] He got there unnoticed because, he said, 'I adopted the same principle that enabled me to conceal my whereabouts so long in Ireland. I always watch the other fellow instead of letting him watch me. I make a point of keeping the other fellow on the run, instead of being on the run myself. That is the secret of success which I have learned during the past year or two'.[9] He used an assumed name and with a friend slipped unnoticed into a taxicab.

The Irish delegation, headed by Arthur Griffith, took two houses – at 22 Hans Place and at 15 Cadogan Gardens, where Mick stayed. The first meeting took place on 11 October. That morning he scribbled a note to Kitty: 'Of all the times in God's world, do you know when I'm writing this? Almost 4 o'clock in the morning.'[10]

When he got no response from Kitty he sent her a telegram. 'Someone here very disappointed at not hearing ... '[11]

Kitty had to untangle the web which she had woven.

For the moment she continued to keep the two lovers on a string. She cabled a message to Harry in New York. Harry 'was delighted' with the cable, and said, 'I am eagerly looking forward to next Monday's mail to hear from you and praying that you will have written to say you are coming!'

He tried to impress on her the importance she had for him. 'We [friends] were out tonight sightseeing and I was thinking how nice 'twould be if you were here. Life would be so pleasant in this wonderful land. So come along at once like an angel and we will be for ever happy.'[12] This letter from Harry was written on the same day that Mick and his comrades were attending the first meeting of the conference at 10 Downing Street.

Mick also wrote to Kitty and told her he lit 'a very big' candle for her after Mass. He had done the same the previous day. This morning he wrote: 'I did a journey of five miles to my sister's place for a letter from you – no letter. Honestly, I felt it terribly, but I do not believe that you have failed to write, and won't believe it until I know.'

Kitty's sister Helen and Paul McGovern were on their honeymoon, and Mick met them with other friends for dinner and a show afterwards. 'I'd have given anything to have had you there. Alas!' He said he even 'kind of told Helen' about his plans – that Kitty and he should have a life together. 'I fancy they'd all be very pleased – What do you think?' Briefly his thoughts turned to the negotiations. 'Tough work before me.'[13]

A few days later Harry sent Kitty the speech he was to deliver in New York, 'so that you may read it,' he wrote. He wanted her to feel as if she were in the audience. Soon he would travel to Washington and then Chicago to deliver the speech. He wished she were there but expected he would not have too long to wait.

Mick also continued to write to Kitty. On 13 October he apologised for getting 'into a state of great concern' when he hadn't received her letters. 'I want you to know that you are in my mind, and I think of you every moment I am free.' He asked her to bear with his impatience. 'You will often be called on to stand a lot from me. *But then straightforwardness and understanding*' are needed.

He did not resent her 'sermon ... I have often felt that it required someone like you to make me appreciate the thing properly ... Always write as you feel, to me at any rate. I'll do the same to you'. In a footnote he wrote, 'We must, I think, make that arrangement more binding, but just as you desire. I feel somehow that it will work out and work out well'.[14]

Across the Atlantic in New York, Harry had similar thoughts. He wrote that his principal base would be with the O'Mara family who had gone to the US to assist de Valera in 1920. 'Of course I will be lonely until I know you are coming,' Harry wrote, 'and I will not give you an hour's rest until you have landed here ... with fond love to you, sweetheart ... Your devoted lover, Harry.'[15]

That same morning Mick wrote to Kitty from London. He had just returned from Mass where he had lit a candle for Kitty. He takes her to task for her little 'rebuke about someone else ... You are the one – never fear. How I wish I could see you now and have one of those lovely serious talks with you. They are the best ones, aren't they?' He told her that the previous day's conference was 'the hardest day yet from early morning until eight almost.'[16]

That night, after his long day's work of negotiation, he took a short walk and sat down to reply to her 'very lovable' letters which he got at lunch time. He said he had read them 'many times since'.

'I do think I am quite certain of the relationship and I just loved the way you stated the case. So like you – I'm always thinking now that we shall get on better and better – what do you think?' He left the letter unfinished. Next day he resumed it 'at 4.15 in the afternoon after a fearful hard

102

slogging day'. He was feeling tired 'but happy also' as he had caught up with his arrears of work. He assured Kitty he was wearing the tie which she sent him and said she could see it in the photo he was enclosing. He responded to her query about travelling to London – he would love to have her but warned her that she 'wouldn't get much attention' because of his busy schedule.[17]

Harry sent 'a hurried note' from New York and told of the 'wonderful welcome' he got at Madison Square. But life wasn't full without Kitty. He was due to leave for Washington but, he told Kitty, he had an intense longing for her. He was 'thinking of you all the time and wishing you were with me. Hurry along and enjoy the great Indian Summer in this wonderful land. I prayed on your beads at Mass this morning for you, and I know you said a wee prayer for me. Write often ... Your devoted lover, Harry.'[18]

Mick wrote a long letter to Kitty on 16 October: 'Was at two Masses today! One in my usual Oratory 8 o'c. The other an official one at Maiden Lane. Even at the official one I managed to come back and light a candle for you. Second one therefore, today.'

Mick was glad that he had found favour with Paul and her sister, Helen. 'Every test passed is another milestone on the way to life-long happiness,' he wrote.[19]

Harry, from New York, stressed to Kitty: 'I will not go to California until you come, and as there is a pressing demand for me out there I put it up to you as a national question to come at once ... May God bless and guard you is the prayer of – your fond lover, Harry'.[20]

In London Mick wasn't enamoured of the publicity he was getting – 'all the praise and flattery that has been showered on me since I came here ... You will know I hope that they [journalists] leave me untouched just as their dispraise and their blame did. All the same to me'.[21]

Next day he again wrote to Kitty: 'Just a line – only a

line to wish you well and to let you know I am thinking of you Yesterday's photograph has been published, I am told – *Nervous Michael Collins*'.[22]

Meanwhile Harry was writing to Kitty that he was 'back on the job in great shape ... I have not dared to tell them [Seán Nunan and the boys] of my great hope, and I will spring your coming as a great surprise'.[23]

Because of Mick's high profile Kitty wonders how life in London is for him – 'Meet any nice girls that you liked? Did you kiss anybody since? I didn't – didn't get the chance (You know I'm only joking!) I too wish I could see you, to have one of those great little chats. They certainly are great'.

She tells him: 'I'm a moody creature sometimes, but I don't think you are ... You are just yourself when with me. I wonder if I'm always myself with you. Of course I do want to be'. She couldn't be herself fully while she was stringing Harry along as well, but this she kept a secret from Mick. She told Mick she prayed for him at Mass and reminded him that the lighted candle was her idea.[24] Indeed, she was also praying for Harry, and praying for herself, about her decision.

Mick was in a jumpy mood in his next letter to Kitty. He said he had been 'very cross' when writing the previous letter. He tried 'hard' to forget her, 'but it wouldn't work out'. The reason he wanted to forget her was due to the 'severe letter' which she had written him; now he hoped she wouldn't write 'any more severe letters'. He agreed that without her he would never have thought of the candles, 'I know that you have been of immense help to me'. Nor did he intentionally mean his letters to 'fall short ... But life has to take in the serious things as well as the light things, and even though we may like sunshine always, it is not practical nor indeed – and remember this – is it desirable? *And that's that!*' he concluded.[25]

He was shouldering the burden of difficult negotiations and the problems of trying to ensure Kitty's affections. The previous night he 'escaped' from everybody and went for a drive alone. 'Rather funny – the great M. C. in lonely splendour. I am lonely actually and I suppose you won't believe that, *and that's that*.'[26] Kitty's next letter did not bring him joy. He felt she was expecting too much of their relationship and certainly had a sense that she was creating difficulties not in order to make things work but to give herself an escape route:

> Don't be putting up too severe tests. Don't attempt to walk before we have learned to crawl. That is a fatal mistake ... Do you know how your letter strikes me ... that you are trying to get out of it. I want it to work out and I promise to do my part of it. If it's not possible, then God help us, but let us have a fair chance.[27]

If he was in jail and couldn't write, he told her, he wouldn't forget her, so why should he forget her now – not because he was far away! 'If you only knew the difficulty I have in finding time, you'd know how unfair you were to talk of long letters. (Since I commenced this, I have had to deal with several business letters, a few callers and a few phone calls.)' Though he felt she was angry with him, yet:

> I would not change a word in your letter for I don't like gramophone effects. *I like people to say what they themselves think and mean* ... If it [the relationship] can't last through misfortune and trouble and difficulty and unpleasantness and age then it's no use. In riches and beauty and pleasure it is so easy to be quite all right. That is no test though.[28]

The next day he gave her a flavour of his busy schedule:

> Have been working all the morning and now I'm rushing for the Conference. Am keeping them late *as usual*, they say, and you say I'm neglectful and forgetful if I don't write long letters and so I'm getting into trouble everywhere and that's always my fate.[29]

By this time Kitty appeared to have decided which man she wanted. Mick – Mícheál as he now liked to call himself – asked Kitty some pointed questions, and she said she wasn't displeased:

> I know how you feel about the Harry business ... It is wise what you say about H. etc. I haven't written yet [to Harry]. I don't know exactly what to say. I wish you were here, it would be so much easier to discuss it ... I told H. I didn't love him, and he was prepared to risk it with the idea that I might grow to love him, and I think I told you all the other little things before.

Kitty in this letter said she was being frank with Mick that it was her fault and he shouldn't blame himself in 'the slightest'. 'The agreement that we be absolutely frank is good and should keep all misunderstanding away.'[30]

In a further letter Kitty again mentions Harry. She wants the air cleared and says that the relationship between two people has to be right, love should be built on 'a splendid foundation'. 'I may be wrong,' she told Mick, 'but I think H. is capable of deeper affection (for me) than most men, but he also knows that I don't love him ... This is a very personal letter, and I hope you will forgive me and understand ... I always wanted to make you feel happy, otherwise I would have kept away from you, knowing the danger.'[31]

We have no access to any further letters between Harry and Kitty, nor is there further mention of Harry in any of the letters between Mick and Kitty at this juncture, but she tells Mick that her feelings for him were much stronger than what she felt for Harry. 'Yes, what you say is right, to be straight and understanding. I feel I always want to be straight with you.'

We do not know how Kitty dealt with Harry but it is obvious that she had decided the triangle was ended. By this stage Kitty is full of apologies to Mick; she says he misread her last letter:

You are everything to me, and surely you know it. Then why should I want to hurt you? ... I am sorry. Please forget it and remember that I am always thinking of you. You are never out of my heart ... It worries me and it is always worrying that you have so much to do. Is there no remedy?[32]

With his personal life as with his military and political life he insisted on clarity: 'Please,' he wrote to Kitty, 'always say to me what you think, not what I'd like you to think. That's the only way to get at a proper understanding, and if I don't like what you say, then it's my look-out'.[33]

Now that she has decided in his favour she asks him to come for the weekend: 'Ah, yes try, try ... Write and say we are as great as ever ... Good-bye with my love and a big kiss (if you'll have it). Yours ever, Kit'.[34]

In a later note: 'I'd love to have you here, but we must be really good, no bedroom scene etc. etc. etc. Tuigeann tu? You'll come to me before I go to London perhaps?'[35]

She was going to a dance with a Cavan boy, only seventeen, she tells him, so he won't be jealous. She teases him: 'I'm wearing my old long frock, black and very low! Of course you would be shocked!'[36]

The following day she sends him an account of the dance; she danced all night, 'never sat it out for a second, never felt inclined,' and had only two hours in bed and couldn't sleep. Her 'little black evening dress held up on the shoulders by two little black straps and willpower, no sleeves, long draped skirt with a small slit in front. I felt I never looked so well, and was wishing that you were here to tell me if you liked me ... You like black in evening dresses. It suits me, I think ... . Last night I was yours absolutely, that is if you were perfectly satisfied.' She was determined that this was going to work: 'I want you to know that I love you'.[37]

Mick did get home that weekend and Kitty got to Dublin for 'a great reunion'. He had to get some of the lads to see her home safely as he had to rush for the mailboat back to

London on Sunday night. On the journey he dropped her a brief note: 'I wish you were with me now. It's so lonely, and it's so sad being far away. But then you are with me, aren't you? Why wasn't I so much nicer to you. Good bye Kit, my Kit'.[38]

The next morning he wrote her a quick note before going to Mass, but felt compelled to write to her again later. He had got her letter about the dance. 'You must have been "stunning" looking ... Sounded somewhat on the naked side in reality.' He was concerned about her health, as she had complained to him that she hadn't been feeling well. He suggested a number of doctors and also that she have her sight checked. 'You must take real care of yourself.'[39]

On 24 October, Mick got Mrs Fionán Lynch, who was looking after the female staff on the delegation, to wire Kitty to come to London next day. When she didn't respond he got Mary Duggan to wire twice. He had no time during the day as he was immersed in the negotiations. Kitty agreed and next day travelled to London. There she met her sister Helen and both met Mick the next day.

Because of the demands on his time Mick depended on others to make Kitty's stay enjoyable. One day he asked Kathleen Napoli MacKenna, one of the secretaries, to accompany the Kiernan sisters on a shopping expedition. They were each to select a gift for which he would pay. Kitty selected a smart woollen dress. Kathleen McKenna said, 'Mick, who was very much in love with Kitty, was a proud man as he left Cadogan Gardens with a sister on each arm'.[40]

Mick could give time to Kitty only in the evenings but even these snatches of time Mick said were 'wonderful'. He went to great trouble to see that Gearóid O'Sullivan escorted Kitty to Holyhead and back home safely. 'I have just said that rosary for you,' he wrote afterwards. 'Do you remember our words about my being sorry that I hadn't been nice to you? Well, I must say it again ... I pray you not to be too hard on me for you know how difficult my task is and, as I said before, I visit my nastiness on my best friends.'[41]

Every morning Mick was up between 6 and 6.30. He went to Mass, at which he would light a candle for Kitty. Afterwards he would write a note to her at some stage while having his breakfast, reading letters, dealing with correspondence, having a political chat with his comrades, then spending a long day at intense conference meetings. In the evenings there was so much to discuss with the delegation that each moment was crammed with activity.

Ned Broy, who had been released from Arbour Hill and whom Mick had brought over as his private secretary, got uneasy about his early morning absence from the house, so he followed him unseen one morning. He discovered his daily Mass routine. Mick confided in Kitty that the early morning walk to Brompton Oratory was refreshing. Being alone with himself and his God gave him peace of mind for a short space.

London Society and Conferences

As October drew to a close, major issues were on the conference table: the unity of Ireland, allegiance to the crown, common citizenship, naval defence, the national debt, war pension, compensation, and tariffs. Being under an obligation to maintain secrecy, Mick did not mention any of the difficulties or lengthy discussions in his letters to Kitty, only '– lovely day – bells ringing for Church and Chapel – sunshine on left, typewriters clacking on my right. I have kept the lovely secretaries in working, and it's a shame for me, but alas I have to do it'.[1]

Not long after he arrived in London, he had sent James Douglas to America to ascertain whether the new state would be in a position to borrow without complete fiscal autonomy. Douglas informed him that Harry Boland was preparing American opinion to accept a resumption of hostilities. Even at this point, the mindset of the two men was diverging.

Arthur Griffith, who was not in great health, asked Mick to act as unofficial leader of the delegation and Mick, who had always admired Griffith, agreed to take on this extra burden.

From the outset the delegates were a disunited group, with tensions that had previously existed within the cabinet becoming magnified. Throughout the period of de Valera's absence in America Mick remained loyal to him, but when the Stack/Brugha axis dominated cabinet views on his visits to Dublin, Mick sensed that seeds of dissension were being sown. The unease between de Valera and himself would simmer from this on.

In the evenings he would get away from the group to drop around to his sister Hannie. She would have news of home or of Sister Celestine and he could chat to her about his plans for a life with Kitty.

He disliked seeing his photographs in newspapers, and Kitty's description of his 'Charlie Chaplin moustache' did not help. He would have to get rid of that! Now he knew that if the war was renewed, his cover was blown: he could not hide. His four years in the secret life of espionage was poor preparation for the notoriety that was now visited on him.

After only a few weeks into the discussions Mick was acutely aware of the difficulties and the contrast between his own soldierly style and the machinations of politicians. He was confronted with 'a real nest of singing birds'. He told John O'Kane on 23 October that 'they chirrup mightily one to the other – and there's the falseness of it all, because not one trusts the other. Lloyd George's attitude I find to be particularly obnoxious,' he wrote. 'He is all comradely – all craft and wiliness – all arm around shoulder – all the old friends act ... Not long ago he would joyfully have had me at the rope end. He thinks that the past is all washed out now – but that's to my face. What he thinks behind my back makes me sick at the thought of it.'[2]

He soon realised that what they were being offered was 'not freedom but the power to achieve freedom'. Unlike de Valera, symbols were not important to him; but both he and Griffith fought for the acceptance of de Valera's External Association plan. He began to observe that the best they could do was to get some temporary settlement. 'You cannot create a republic overnight,' he wrote to John O'Kane.[3] (It is believed that 'John O'Kane' is a pseudonym Collins used for a friend – his exact identity remains unknown.)

He made a quick trip home in early November, with some of the other delegates. Despite the secrecy that they tried to observe, the newspapers carried rumours of a crisis. Mark Sturgis noted in his diary: 'Collins was seen this morning talking to Mulcahy in the hall of the Gresham and words portending war have been reported to me'.[4]

He paid a short visit to Granard. 'As usual when I got back

111

to town,' he wrote to Kitty afterwards, 'there were several people looking for me and a meeting.' He found the weekend did him 'a great deal of good. The constant and changing fresh air was a great tonic'.[5]

The meeting that Sunday evening was an electric one. Ernie O'Malley and some of the Tipperary battalion officers had been summoned to the Gresham Hotel for an enquiry into the seizure of rifles by the IRA. Collins was very concerned about this breach of the truce and angry when he met the men: 'Some of you bloody fellows know about this, The rifles did not walk away. Negotiations in London will be held up over a few rifles. The British will say we have broken faith'. He shook his head, tossed his hair back from his forehead: 'Come on, by Christ, and answer the question I ask.'

Afterwards Eoin O'Duffy apologised for him. 'I'm sorry he lost his temper, but he is very worried and we cannot blame him.' O'Duffy told them that there were difficulties in the negotiations on the oath of allegiance issue. 'If they end suddenly, it will be due to the seizure of the rifles,' as the British team would be 'glad of an excuse'.[6]

Lawless activities had begun to break the peace in many parts of Ireland. Men who had been on active service for so long over the previous few years now found it hard to settle into the dull routine of work.

But there were breaches also on the British side. Griffith drew attention to a British GHQ circular conveying to the police that the negotiations were due to break and they should be prepared for ruthless 'hunting down of the rebels'. Sir Laming Worthington-Evans, secretary of state for war, denied the existence of such a document. Collins retorted: '*We know*. You can't issue these documents without my knowledge'. He said that the department had circulated a photograph of himself for police purposes, and also that a British detective watched him while he attended Mass.[7]

On 8 November, the morning after the Dublin meeting,

The young Collins with his sister, Mary (Collins-Powell),
his Granny O'Brien and his mother, Marianne

Sinead Mason, Collins' secretary

Dilly Dicker with some of the trinkets Collins gave her

The Daly family in 1901

(left to right) front row: Aileen, Kathleen, Madge, Ned – back row: Nora, Annie, Agnes, Carrie, Laura

Madge Daly before the First World War

Kathleen Clarke in 1923

Madge Hales

Josephine Barrett

Peg (left) and Dell Barrett with friends

Collins with Emmet Dalton,
Portobello Barracks, 1922

Collins in 1917

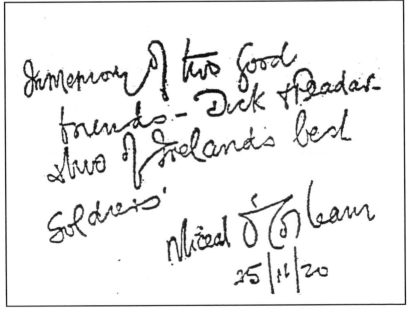

Collins' message on the wreath of Dick McKee and Peader Clancy,
November 1920

Stafford
June 17th 16

My Dear Susan

It seems ages + ages since
I wrote you and I have been wondering
for about the past fortnight why in the
world you haven't written — and in fact I
made two efforts. Did you get them?
I hope there is nothing wrong anyway.
It seems likely that we are going to a
camp from this place next week or so
Somewhere in N Wales near Bala. Nothing
has been told us definitely. There, we shall
have possibly a better time, more room at
all events. Very cold in all probability so
I can promise plenty of begging. Will let
you know in due course. For the present I wonder
if you'd mind sending me a cap size 7 — very plain
dark grey if poss and a tie any colour but also plain
Really + truly I don't like asking people for things. One
has to in this place though. Gilheart + the Nunans
are all very well.
Love
Michael Collins

Michael Collins to Susan Killeen
from Stafford detention centre, June 1916

Clockwise from top:
Kitty Kiernan, Susan
Killeen, Dilly Dicker,
Michael Collins, Nancy
O'Brien, Lady Hazel
Lavery, Moya Llewelyn
Davies

he arrived back in London after an extremely rough crossing; he slept on the train, 'turned in for about 2 hours, up at 7.30, Mass at 8,' after which he lit a candle for Kitty. 'Yes indeed,' he told her, 'I'm thinking so very much of you now.'

Once back in London he plunged into work, and on Tuesday morning in his short note to Kitty he told her about 'a clamour' which was for him 'to attend to certain things'. However, he felt he had a little leeway as he 'let everybody go off last night and stayed alone in the house. Worked steadily for three or four hours'.[8]

On 15 November, James Douglas reported to him from New York that 'there is plenty of money here to be lent to Ireland, if there is peace, but I am afraid the big men will not take the loan otherwise ... '[9] The stark reality for Collins was that should the negotiations break down and warfare resume, Ireland must plough on alone. On the same day the British team handed their draft proposals for a treaty to the Irish delegation.

Mick made a short boat trip to Dublin with the proposals but had to rush back again. 'I was called back specially last night,' he wrote to Kitty on 15 November. 'I had nearly wired you asking you to come up on the night train. Lucky I didn't for I'd have had to come [return] in any case and then you'd have found fault.' He felt torn between the demands she made on him and his other demands – 'Mr G. [Griffith] is waiting for me and so will the other G. [L. George].'

A mention of Harry Boland in this letter suggests that Mick feels he is still in the picture as far as Kitty is concerned.

He was not a man for brooding, not even about the intrigue of the 'Dublinites' as he termed them, and he advised Kitty not to brood unnecessarily on her personal problems. 'If one broods over a thing one is very likely to give it an importance it doesn't deserve, and a doubt cultivated is apt to flourish exceedingly.'[10]

Erskine Childers now proved to be a thorn in Collins'

side: he was distrusted by the English as a hardliner on the delegation, and Collins suspected him of feeding extremist views back to de Valera. He wrote to O'Kane: 'Who should one trust – even on my own side of the fence? Beyond Griffith, no one'.[11]

The pressure was great, he told Kitty, 'I'd write several times, if I could – but you won't realise what I have on hand'.[12] Next day, 16 November, he took a breather from a meeting of the delegation, 'Up very late last night and in a ferment of haste and worry all the day ... I don't think I've been a single hour away from work.'[13] His life was to become even more difficult.

Hazel Lavery had met Michael Collins at parties during his early London days. She had taken a great interest in Irish affairs because of her Irish ancestry and her friendship with Moya Llewelyn Davies – regarding herself, according to her husband, as an 'Irish girl'. In an attempt to promote the idea of Home Rule for Ireland, Sir John Lavery had painted portraits of Nationalist leader John Redmond and Unionist leader Edward Carson, and stipulated that the paintings should be hung together in a Dublin gallery. Hazel believed that an 'Irish Collection' would help Irish reconciliation.

After the Rising, Sir John attended the trial of Roger Casement, accompanied by Hazel, and painted the scene. He offered the painting for sale on behalf of Kathleen Clarke's National Aid Society. The 1916 executions and contact with the relatives of the leaders had a profound effect on Hazel. Again, during the War of Independence she was horrified by newspaper reports about the atrocities committed by the Black and Tans. In October 1920 the Laverys came to Ireland on a painting trip. The War of Independence was at its height and Hazel decided that from then on she would make Irish freedom her principal interest. When she met Lloyd George at Philip Sassoon's house she pleaded for a change in British policy. Also in 1920 she converted to Catholicism – her husband and her daughter by her first marriage, Alice Trudeau, were already Catholics.[14]

> According to her husband she loved making friends:
> She had the gift, and the power to use it delighted her always. She enjoyed all sorts and conditions of people, and she was almost childishly anxious to win each and everyone's esteem and affection. She was genuinely interested in all she met ... all humanity enthralled her – she was in love with the spectacle of life ... her life was life itself ... She had much Irish blood, but she was primarily an American aristocrat.

Since Mick first met Hazel he had been fascinated by her lively mind. 'Her views on books were found so worthwhile even by Bernard Shaw that he used to send her batches of his *Intelligent Woman's Guide to Socialism* while he was writing it. But,' her husband wrote, 'it was as a hostess that she excelled and found her true art. She had exquisite tact and discrimination, and mixed her friends with the ease and grace of the most successful diplomat.'

When the Treaty negotiations started Hazel suggested that her husband, who had spent some time previously painting in Connemara, should 'do something' for Ireland. He agreed to make his studio a 'neutral ground where both sides might meet' and so it became a venue for many fruitful discussions. It was really at this time that the handsome and enigmatic Michael Collins, who was at ease in all situations, won the admiration of Hazel. This admiration of him continued while he lived.[15]

Because of Collins' fame Hazel was anxious that her husband should paint his portrait. He had already painted de Valera's portrait during his London negotiations in July. Now in November Hazel got in touch with Michael's sister, Hannie. This brought all the delegation in turn to Sir John Lavery's studio for sittings.

Collins walked into the studio one morning – 'a tall young Hercules with a pasty face, sparkling eyes, and a fascinating smile'. Sir John 'helped him off with a heavy overcoat to which he clung, excusing himself by saying casually, "There is a gun in the pocket."'

Sir John observed he was 'a patient sitter' who liked 'to sit facing the door ... always on the alert'.[16] Mick himself found it 'absolute torture,' he told Kitty, 'I was expected to keep still, and this, as you know, is a thing I cannot do'.[17]

Hazel got to know all the delegates, but had a particular liking for Mick Collins. She was anxious that the Irish group 'should meet Englishmen of importance concerned with the Irish question, and this resulted in many dinner-parties and other functions'. Despite all her persuasive powers she could not induce Erskine Childers to come to her home, 'not even for a meal,' her husband wrote.[18]

Her husband welcomed the influential people she took it upon herself to entertain. Her home at Cromwell Place soon became 'a centre of activity' for this political group. Mick Collins and Arthur Griffith 'met intimately, men like Lord Birkenhead, Winston Churchill and Lord Londonderry, and were able to talk things over in a friendly way as they could have done nowhere else,' according to Elizabeth Countess of Fingall, Lady Lavery's cousin. She remembers 'so many interesting lunches and dinners at that house, with usually some important significance behind them. Dinner was often in Sir John's studio upstairs, which made such a delightful background'. The countess innocently believed that 'it might be said truly that the Irish Treaty was framed and almost signed at 5 Cromwell Place'.[19]

One night at dinner Hazel, at the end of the table, had Michael Collins on one side and Field-Marshal Lord French, ex Irish viceroy, on the other. Lord French looked across and said, 'This is the first time I have had the pleasure of meeting you, Mr Collins'.

116

'It is not the first time I have seen your Lordship,' said Collins. 'For a couple of months ago you were by yourself near the Lodge and the boys surrounded you; but I called them off.' (Collins, who had organised the ambush, called it off because the train arrived ahead of schedule.)

'London,' said French, 'is the best place, after all, to meet people. For a considerable time I was on the heels of De Wet in South Africa and only caught up with him in London here, at dinner.'[20]

According to Oliver St John Gogarty:

> Dinner at the Laverys brought you into the company of persons of incalculable importance. A house which was welcomed as an unofficial meeting-place for rebel and ruler was of inestimable use and service to both sides – Ireland and England. Without it what is the picture? Mr Collins makes his statement to the powers that be, and is answered with all the stiffness which such statements must have for the followers who put each side into power by utterances ... At 5, Cromwell Place men would meet as human beings beyond the scent of herded wolves, and exchange views and reveal difficulties. Arthur Griffith was grateful for this accommodation. The Laverys did more to bring about a settlement than all the weary official and overworked weeks at Hans Place.[21]

Collins was conscious of being misinterpreted, and also of his image. Emmet Dalton approved of his decision not to drink alcohol during any of the lunches or dinners. 'Mick was shrewd – always a step ahead. The Laverys were well connected with the people who mattered ... Mick, as director of intelligence, knew he could get inside information, and he did, through Hazel.'[22]

At lunch one day Lord Birkenhead was a guest. During the meal Hazel's small Peke dog was under the table and began pawing at Lord Birkenhead. Hazel realised this, and called the little dog. 'Oh, I am sorry,' said Lord Birkenhead. 'I though you were making advances.'

Fuming, Collins jumped up. 'D'ye mean to insult her?'

Hazel, wishing to calm the situation, said, 'Lord Birkenhead was only joking.'

'I don't understand such jokes,' said an irate Mick.[23]

Back at the conference table each day brought its own problems. Lloyd George soon saw the cracks among the Irish delegation. Griffith had an intense hatred for Childers, whom he called 'that damned Englishman'. But the closeness between the cousins Barton and Childers meant that Collins and Griffith had to exclude Barton from their most private deliberations during some of the discussions. It created a difficulty for Collins as Barton had been Collins' comrade and he had thought highly of him during the last four years of war.

There was stalemate. Any decision on the issue of the crown must be referred to Dublin, according to de Valera's instructions, and he had already said this could mean war. The British delegation on the other hand had made it clear that without recognition of the crown there could be no settlement.

Collins was utterly dismayed. 'Dublin is the real problem,' he wrote to O'Kane. 'They know what we are doing, but I don't know exactly the state of their activities. No turning back now.'[24] He told O'Kane of his concern for Griffith's health, and the strain he was under.

As head of the delegation, Griffith was led into a trap. In return for promises of a Boundary Commission, he gave Lloyd George his 'personal assurances' on the Crown, unknown to the others, in writing – a useful weapon for Lloyd George which he would use to his own advantage later on.

On 22 November the Irish delegation handed their draft proposal to the British team, 'upon the assumption that the essential unity of Ireland is maintained'.

It added to Mick's problems that the 'Dublinites' (as he called them) had decided to play their own game. Brugha, minister of defence, was still sanctioning the collection of arms

118

for the IRA. Early in November he had sent Michael Hogan and Ned Lynch to London to buy arms with instructions to steer clear of Collins and Sam Maguire. One evening Ned Lynch got a message that Collins wished to see him. Collins confronted him – on whose orders was he purchasing arms? 'If this Treaty isn't signed you'll have more guns than men to use them. Things are being made difficult for us over here – don't make them more so,' said 'The Big Fellow', who then shook hands and walked away.[25]

Nevertheless, within a few days there was a daring raid on Windsor Barracks, with 'inside' help. Lynch and a comrade were captured but the others got away with the arms. The IRA admitted their involvement.

This hit the negotiations hard. If the IRA were involved Michael Collins had to be behind it, according to Field-Marshal Sir Henry Wilson. He was convinced also that Collins was behind the other raids in Ireland even though he was continuing to engage in negotiations. Now Collins was in a no-win situation. Cathal Brugha had succeeded. Before he sent over the men he knew Collins would have to take the rap. 'There was little Collins could do for his hands were securely tied, the mesh of intrigue roped tightly about him.'[26]

LETTERS – IN GREAT HASTE

'We have been at it in a most serious fashion all today,' Mick wrote to Kitty on 24 November, and shortly after he ominously said that the 'position is very serious and I may be returning with anything but satisfactory news'. He agonised. He had been thrown into this pit and he had to find his way out.

He knew that concessions on both sides would be required, and that the gap was wide on the main questions of allegiance to the crown and Ulster. The delegation had to put aside the question of Ulster in order to deal first with the knotted allegiance problem.

Back in Dublin on the weekend of 25 November, he attended a cabinet meeting which began at three o'clock and was still in progress at seven. Brugha and Stack were openly hostile to Collins and tried to use Mulcahy to attack him.[1]

It was late before this meeting closed, and Mick needed further discussion with Mulcahy and others, but in between he snatched a moment to drop a line to Kitty; he expressed the hope that he could 'get away tomorrow night to Granard, but things are most awfully uncertain, it's quite on the cards that I may have to return to London ... in great haste, Mícheál.'[2]

Next day Mick attended a long fiery meeting of the IRB Supreme Council. He knew he would encounter problems with Brugha and Stack no matter what 'deal' they brought back, and he realised that what was being offered would not please de Valera either – these men distrusted the IRB, and distrusted himself, he knew.

The day was crowded with activity. He got to Granard, but had to return in Joe Hyland's waiting car to make the night boat back to England. He tried to fit in a normal life between his numerous activities but his time for courtship had become less and less. He wanted Kitty to understand him:

'I'm greatly afraid you see the worst side of me,' he wrote to her on 28 November.[3]

He found consolation in her letters, which he told her he read over and over again silently late into the night. On 30 November, alone, sitting up in bed after a hard day he reread all her letters, he told her, then tried to write to her but had to give up. 'Positively I was too worn out to write legibly.' But he was up again early for Mass, lit a candle for Kitty, and began to write to her before breakfast.

He expressed his concern for the stress his precarious 'appointments must make' on her time. 'But how can I help it?' he pleaded. 'I didn't have a minute more than you know of. If you can realise this, what does it matter if people do make suggestions like you say they did?' The innuendos that he referred to were that he was seeing another woman, Lady Hazel Lavery. 'I don't find it very agreeable sometimes, I assure you, and I don't find the forced absence very pleasant,' he wrote. He was 'in a very troubled state of mind' that morning. 'Troubled about many things,' he said, not least her 'lack of understanding.'[4]

Many difficulties arose as the debates progressed. Because of Griffith's poor health, Collins, the unofficial leader, shouldered much responsibility. In a letter to his friend John O'Kane he wrote: 'He [Griffith] and I recognise that if such a thing were official [Collins as unofficial leader] it would provide bullets for the unmentionables'. The topic of the Dublinites was discussed between Griffith and himself 'for the thousandth time'.[5]

Collins found time to renew acquaintance with some old friends from his early London days but there was a tinge of sadness in his visits to his long-time friend and fellow west Cork man, Tom Hales in Pentonville. Despite being under surveillance, he did succeed, speaking some Irish, in conveying to Hales the difficulties of getting a Republic from the British. Hales was very special to him; it was a friendship

121

that went very far back. Hales had suffered greatly; he was one of the few held in jail after the Truce and Collins, try as he might, failed to get him released.

Mick walked the London streets alone. Apart from his letters to Kitty there is no record of his thoughts, of his emotions, or of his turmoil as he tramped to and from his Cadogan Garden lodgings, while somewhere in the background Ned Broy kept a watchful eye.

On 1 December, Griffith and Collins got the British leaders to agree that Ireland should have the same status as Canada in 'law, practice and constitutional' usage, which was more in line with Childers' view.

Mick drafted a quick line to Kitty, told her not to fuss about his cold which she observed he had when last she met him. He thought he might be going to Dublin for the weekend, but because of the pressure didn't think he'd have a chance to meet her.[6]

He received her letter on 2 December. She said, 'You know by this time how anxious I am to secure your love really well, and how I long for this more than anything else, so much so that it must bore you sometimes. With me nothing seems to matter except that love between the two of us.' She asked him to forgive her if she periodically expresses doubt. 'You are the first who made me believe in love, and that's why I wouldn't like to be ever disappointed in you.' She admitted that it was probably 'silly' of her to express doubts and desires; she realised, she said, that he was much more 'sensible'.[7]

Next day he got another letter from Kitty acknowledging his. 'I really probably misunderstood you ... I am happy to drift and drift as long as I know you love me and we will be one day together. I fancy sometimes – as girls do – a nest, you and I, two comfy chairs, a fire, and two books (now I'm not too ambitious) and no worries. You feeling perfectly free, as if not married, and I likewise ... All I wish now is that it pleases you, gives you some sunshine, and helps to make the day easy for you. That will always be my ambition.'[8]

Mick felt that the life they both longed for was being smothered by duty to 'the cause'. On 3 December at 7 pm Mick was 'just waiting' while some of the secretaries were agreeing to a report at 10 Downing Street, so he wrote a note to Kitty. 'I have had a most awful day – conferring all the time and I am preparing to clear off now for Euston where I hope to post this, and to see you again.' However, he didn't get away from Downing Street in time for the post.

Later Childers and he had a rough crossing. The boat in which they were travelling ran into another boat, three men were killed and they had 'to put back' to shore.

After this turbulent sleepless night, cold and hungry from the boat trip, he attended a cabinet meeting in the Mansion House on Saturday morning where each of the plenipotentiaries gave his view of the draft terms of the treaty. Brugha created what Childers termed 'an unpleasant scene', and said that the British delegation 'selected their men' by having 'sub-conferences'.[9]

Griffith, furious, demanded a withdrawal of the accusation. Brugha refused. Collins held his temper, and in a measured tone said: 'If you are not satisfied with us, get another five to go over'.[10]

Barton came to the defence and Brugha eventually withdrew his remark. After further accusations and discussions on allegiance to the crown at a meeting which lasted over seven hours, the division within the delegation and within the cabinet was greater than ever.

As Tom Cullen drove Mick back to the boat he complained bitterly of the way he was being treated. 'I've been there all day and I can't get them to say yes or no, whether we should sign or not.'[11] Mick was back in the boat again that night. 'We didn't have time to have tea before we left Dublin,' he wrote to Kitty.[12] They had left the meeting with no clear indication as to what exactly their cabinet colleagues

123

recommended. Barton and Duffy were convinced that the cabinet wanted them to have another attempt at 'External Association' while Collins and Griffith were equally convinced that such was not the decision of the cabinet.[13]

When Collins visited his friends Sir John and Lady Hazel Lavery at 5 Cromwell Place, he was extremely angry and felt he was being pressurised. This was one place where he could freely vent his anger, and it would be helpful if this got back to Lloyd George. Sir John told him that 'he who loses his temper in argument is lost,' but he failed to dissuade him. Eventually, 'after hours of persuasion, Hazel prevailed'.[14]

Still very annoyed because of the confusion in Dublin, he agreed to talk to Lloyd George, only because Griffith appealed to him and because the others had failed. Despite disillusionment he would make a last effort; he wrote to O'Kane that 'the only names worth considering after *this* will be the names of those who have kept away from London ... whichever way it means trouble at home.'[15]

On the morning of 5 December, Collins was still reluctant to meet Lloyd George, and though normally a stickler for punctuality arrived later than the appointed time. He found Lloyd George in a friendly mood, prepared to make concessions provided there was retention of the opening clause of the draft treaty keeping the Free State within the Commonwealth.[16]

In the afternoon Collins, Griffith and Barton returned to Downing Street to discuss the four points (the north-east, defence, trade, the oath). Collins' morning meeting bore fruit; Lloyd George conceded fiscal autonomy. Collins sought this because of its importance to Ireland's borrowing power. The complicated question of the north-east took up much of the afternoon while they awaited a reply on the unity of Ireland from Craig. Collins felt that 'Ireland is Ireland. Borderland is trouble and always will be'.[17]

At the sub-conference Collins suggested that Tyrone, Fermanagh, parts of Derry, Armagh and Down would be saved by the Boundary Commission provided Craig responded positively. And so the arguments dragged on. Collins stated: 'That every document we [the Irish] ever sent them [the British] had stated that any proposal for the association of Ireland with the British Commonwealth of Nations was conditional upon the unity of Ireland. That, unless Craig accepted inclusion under the all-Ireland Parliament, the unity of Ireland was not assured ... '[18]

Lloyd George, seated at the other side of the table, jumped. He accused the Irish delegation of trying to break on the Ulster question. He brandished an envelope and reminded Griffith that a document contained in it had been shown him by Tom Jones [secretary to the British delegation] on 13 November and he [Griffith] had agreed to its contents.

'What is this letter?' Barton whispered to Collins.

'I don't know what the hell it is,' Collins growled.

'Do you mean to tell me, Mr Collins, that you never learnt of this document from Mr Griffith?' A perplexed Collins looked on as the memorandum outlining the Boundary Commission proposal was passed to Barton and himself. Lloyd George said he had fulfilled his part of the bargain. 'Now it is for you to show that Irishmen know how to keep faith.'[19]

'I said I would not let you down on that, and I won't,' Griffith declared.[20]

Other items were agreed, including the oath which Collins had introduced in the morning – an oath the bones of which the IRB had agreed to when last he met them. Finally Arthur Griffith said he would sign the agreement, but added that it would be unfair to expect his colleagues to do so prior to Craig's response.

'Do I understand, Mr Griffith, that though everyone else refuses, you will nevertheless agree to sign?' asked Lloyd George.

'Yes, that is so, Mr Prime Minister.'[21]

Lloyd George replied: 'Every delegate must sign the document and undertake to recommend it, or there can be no agreement ...' He then produced two envelopes. 'I have to communicate with Sir James Craig tonight. Here are the alternative letters which I have prepared ... If I send this letter it is war, and war within three days. Which letter am I to send? Whichever letter you choose travels by special train to Holyhead, and by destroyer to Belfast. The train is waiting with steam up at Euston ... we must have your answer by ten tonight. You can have until then, but no longer to decide whether you will give peace or war to your country.'[22]

As the Irish delegation prepared to leave, Churchill noted that 'Michael Collins rose looking as though he was going to shoot someone, preferably himself. In all my life I have never seen so much pain and suffering in restraint'.

Back in Hans Place, Collins, Childers and the other four delegates fought over whether they would sign for 'Ireland being a dominion and certain peace versus a Republic in some form and apparently certain war'.

They were a divided, overtired, overstrained group of men, although all ready to do what was best for Ireland. Collins had some time previously agreed with Griffith that they were in it together so he was not now likely to desert his colleague; he had indicated as much to Barton as they returned from Downing Street. They talked, argued, shouted, stopped, shouted again and again.

Finally Collins, Griffith and Duggan put on their hats and coats and prepared to go, but Barton and Duffy held them back. Again the argument raged. Mick's mind was made up. He had pointed out to the Irish delegation the difficulty the IRA would have in achieving any success should the war be reactivated. As it stood, the physical force element lacked arms and had lost the coordination and harmony that had taken so many years to achieve. Furthermore it would not have the backing of his own intelligence department as this was now without a cover.

'Do you want to send them out to be slaughtered?' he asked.

This stung Duggan. 'Barton,' said Duggan, 'you will be hanged from a lamp post in Dublin if your refusal to sign causes a new war in Ireland.' He then broke down as he recalled colleagues who had been killed.[23]

Collins headed for Cadogan Gardens. He wanted to let the others tease it out. Later he returned to Hans Place. After a long wait the men came down the stairs. 'All were silent, taut and serious as if walking in a funeral procession.'[24]

Barton had caved in, and Duffy, not prepared for the responsibility of war, consented.

Through a thick fog the men with heavy hearts headed back to Downing Street. There they tried to squeeze some more concessions. After much discussion a few changes were agreed. It was half past two in the morning of 6 December when they consented and signed the Articles of Agreement for a Treaty.

Collins rose. 'I may have signed my political death-warrant tonight,' said Birkenhead, turning to Collins.

'I may have signed my actual death-warrant,' was Collins' prophetic utterance.[25]

LADY LAVERY SPIES
ON BRITISH CABINET

Outside Number 10 Downing Street journalists who had waited in the darkness and in the thick fog saw the delegates emerge. One approached Michael Collins as he swept past. 'Have you anything to say?' he asked.

'Not a word!' growled Collins. He looked tired and upset. Though it was approaching 3 o'clock he headed for Cromwell Place. He wanted to let the Laverys know the distress he felt.

Hazel Lavery saw the torment of the previous few days on his face as she opened the door. He looked 'white and haggard'.[1] In her home he talked very little, Sir John noted. He had acted correctly, he felt; he had weighed it up but now he pondered the consequences.

He knew that back in Ireland there would be those who would welcome the relief, but he knew also that the Treaty fell short of the Republic which he and his comrades had fought so hard for and that this could bring dissent. The confusion which had permeated the recent Dublin cabinet meeting and the ire of Cathal Brugha haunted him.

Hazel Lavery drove him back to Cadogan Gardens. Though tired, he sat and poured his turmoil out on paper to his friend, John O'Kane:

> Think – what have I got for Ireland? Something which she has wanted these past seven hundred years. Will anyone be satisfied at the bargain? Will anyone? I tell you this – early this morning I signed my death warrant. I thought at the time how odd, how ridiculous – a bullet might just as well have done the job five years ago ... These signatures are the first real step for Ireland. If people will only remember that, the first real step.

It was past 5 pm when he flopped on the bed. Two hours later he got out for early Mass. 'Didn't forget your candle' – 'Need I say it!' he told Kitty, picking up the letter he had begun the previous morning – 'what a day I had afterwards!' She was on his mind at this hour. He responded to her concern about their future together.' ... 'Remember that if you ever express doubts I always have that in the back of my mind or indeed very much in the front of my mind. *And that's that.* When you know I think of it in this way don't you feel it gets rid of any necessity to answer your questions in detail?' Her 'lifelong happiness' was important to him, just as his was to her, he argued. But at this remove, he wrote, sadly, '... my plans in regard to home are as yet uncertain.'

'Dearest Kit', he continued. 'I don't know how things will go now but with God's help we have brought peace to this land of ours – a peace which will end this old strife of ours for ever.'[2]

When Tom Cullen met Collins and Griffith at the North Wall, Dublin, on 8 December, Mick seized him by the shoulder, 'Tom, what are our own fellows saying?'

'They're saying what is good enough for Mick, is good enough for me!' he answered. Soon enough Mick would know the truth!

At the Dublin cabinet meeting on 8 December, it became clear that Dev's views had become hardened. Collins was dismayed at 'the open hostility' the delegates faced in the cabinet drawing-room of the Mansion House. De Valera sat gaunt and depressed, Stack was in 'a blazing mood' and Brugha was 'the personification of venom'.

Collins and Griffith had thought that de Valera would support their views, as the Treaty went some way towards satisfying them. They had expected opposition from Brugha and Stack, but not the torrents of accusations which these men hurled at them during the meeting which recessed three times.

De Valera, Brugha and Stack were not prepared to recommend the Articles of Agreement to the Dáil. Finally, after hours of acrimonious dispute, the cabinet endorsed the agreement. A narrow margin separated them – Collins, Griffith, Cosgrave and a reluctant Barton voted in favour, with de Valera, Brugha and Stack against.

Collins left the meeting in extreme distress. He made for Batt O'Connor's, knocked on the door, but remained on the doorstep when Batt opened it. There was a 'strange expression' on his face. 'Come in. What are you waiting for?' asked Batt.

While he still stood there, silent, Batt said, 'Ah, Mick! This is a day I never thought I would live to see'.

'I thought perhaps you would have no welcome for me, Batt,' said Mick.

Agitated he strode up and down the room. 'I will leave Dublin at once,' he said, in extreme bitterness and distress. 'I will go down to Cork. If the fighting is going to be resumed, I will fight in the open, beside my own people down there. I am not going to be chivvied and hunted through Dublin as I have been for the last two years.'

'If we go back to fight, how long could we stick it?' asked Batt.

'A fortnight and it would be over.'

It took some time for Batt to calm him down but eventually he sat down.

The two men talked, had tea and talked and talked until 3 o'clock. Before they parted Mick had assured Batt that he would not leave Dublin. He would see that the Treaty was fully discussed in the Dáil, and put clearly before the people.

'I will accept their verdict,' he said as they parted.[3]

Next morning a letter from de Valera appeared in the public press saying he could not 'recommend the acceptance of this Treaty, either to Dáil Éireann or the country. In this attitude I am supported by the Ministers of Home Affairs and Defence ... ' (Brugha and Stack)[4]

Kathleen O'Connell, de Valera's secretary, had written in her diary on the morning of 8 December: 'P [President] in a awful state. What a fiasco.'[5]

The 'fiasco' took on monstrous proportions as the days passed. To the separatists it became 'a sellout' but to others anxious to get on with daily life, the Treaty was seen as a victory. Soon it was regarded not as the Treaty versus Document Number 2 (de Valera's alternative) but as Michael Collins against de Valera with his two stalwarts, Brugha and Stack.

Mick knew he would face many a friend of old who might no longer be a friend. 'My own brother will probably stand against me in Cork,' he said on that first tortured day. He had not been in touch with Johnny since Johnny's recent release from Spike Island. However, when Johnny came by train to Dublin to meet him, his handshake and smile told all. 'Next time you're shaving, don't overlook that thing,' he said, referring to Mick's moustache. Next morning it was gone.

Collins needed to know what was going on across the water. He was well aware of Hazel Lavery's willingness to convey information. From his years at intelligence gathering he knew what to tell her and what to leave out. She, on the other hand 'was besotted by him and he knew it, he knew he could feed her with the right information and it would get to where he wanted that information to go,' according to Emmet Dalton.[6]

She wrote a letter to Michael which was apparently misdirected and was eventually returned. In a follow-up she wrote that there were so many things more important to him at present than the 'Lost letter of a Lady' and suggested that that would 'make a good title for a romantic novel?':

> The letter is lost I fear and I picture the poor thing wandering desolately about like a pigeon in a storm looking for its owner

131

Mr Michael Collins! and finally bruised and broken, pathetically rejected by man and Post Office, forced to struggle back to Hazel – admittedly a failure, and all its burden of news about perfectly unimportant personal matters having been read by indifferent eyes, alas![7]

Hazel now became the conduit for information from the House of Commons and inside information on the British government. On 9 December she had gone to hear Winston Churchill. His speech 'was very long but excellent,' she wrote, 'and generally well received, excepting of course by the Tories who still rage, albeit more and more powerlessly'.

She wrote:

Today I lunch with Lady Fitzalan [wife of Unionist Chief Whip, Catholic, Lord-Lieutenant of Ireland] and on Tuesday with the Chamberlains' [Austen Chamberlain, leader of the Conservative Party and House of Commons, and member of British Treaty negotiating team].[8]

This had to be interesting news for Collins. On 4 November Collins in a letter to O'Kane had written: 'Don't know why exactly but I don't like Chamberlain ...'[9]

Lady Lavery wrote:

I have not seen L. [the 7th Marquess of Londonderry, a leading Northern Unionist politician] – the other Lord we discussed the other day – as after dinner that night I went home I was so very tired, but I had a talk with Philip [Snowden, Socialist MP] about the matter. He is a clever creature, with imagination and warm towards you (you must get him that dog) also. Thanks to his oriental blood he delights in a secret and he undoubtedly has a certain influence over his illustrious Master' [J. Ramsay MacDonald, Labour leader].

It is obvious that Collins was using Hazel to get information. This letter contained a great deal of substance for Collins. 'That dog' was that code, not a canine he would bring from Ireland. (A code, a key or a cypher was often referred to as a 'dog'). 'I shall not expect an answer,' she wrote, 'unless you tell a secretary to say simply that you have received this letter so that I shall know that it has not gone a-missing.' She adds, 'I *really* mean this *sure*. *Irish sure*. I understand you know. Bless you Michael always. Yours, H'. There appears to be more to this cryptic remark than a surface reading; the Irish word for sure is *cinnte*.

Hazel added a PS. She had found 'a portion of a wonderful book in an old shop'. She would try to get 'an intact copy ... all the facts about the French Revolution' and would send it to him.[10]

A few days later she wrote again to Michael Collins. She had come from the House of Lords where the lord chancellor [the Earl of Birkenhead, Conservative and Treaty negotiator] had been speaking. He had 'replied with his usual devastating urbanity to the bitter but rather futile sarcasm of Carson,' she wrote [Sir Edward Carson, Unionist leader, opponent of Home Rule]. 'All the same the division was a very very close thing for the Gov: only a majority of one!'

Concern by the British cabinet that members of the crown forces were being shot in Ireland was expressed by Winston Churchill who later asked Lady Lavery to 'please write to you [Michael Collins] and say how difficult the incident has made matters here. The old Die Hards have taken a vigorous new lease of life on it. Of course he knows you are doing everything you possibly can, and I hate to write to you and add a further weight of anxiety to your many cares. Please please forgive me'.[11]

Collins had previously asked Hazel to arrange a meeting with the northern Unionist, Lord Londonderry, whom he felt would be in a position to sway Carson towards better north-south relations in Ireland.

She wrote:

In the matter of Lord Londonderry I find rather dissatisfaction. Winston saw him at luncheon and had a long talk but I imagine

from what I have been able to gather not an altogether successful one. Lord L. has intimated that 'he would like to see me
on the subject' and I don't know exactly what that may mean.
Almost anything I should think.[12]

It would be March before Michael Collins and Lord Londonderry would have a face-to-face meeting. (It has been
claimed that Hazel later had a romantic liaison with Lord
Londonderry).[13]

Hazel would often have her letters to Michael Collins
sent via Sir Edward Marsh, one of Churchill's secretaries.
Sam Maguire, Ned Broy and Moya Llewelyn Davies were
emissaries of letters, dispatches and snippets of information
from Hazel to Collins and vice versa.[14]

Collins' letters, according to Shane Leslie's account were
'full of half-educated half-romantic stuff but ending up with
vital messages to the English Cabinet'.[15]

The 'vital messages' were the essential part, the rest a ploy.
The 'vital messages' Hazel would later destroy, the romantic
passages she would keep. An undated fragment believed to be
in Collins' handwriting with certain letters underlined reads:

Hazel, My Dear Dear Hazel,
I too wish it was 'tomorrow' –
With all my love, Yours M.

The 'Yours' is written in a different pen.[16]

'Mick would sometimes lay it on,' according to Emmet
Dalton, especially if letters were posted. 'In fact, as she was
on first name terms with cabinet ministers and entertained
all – what we would call – "the useful people". Mick used the
situation ... We have to remember that intelligence gathering was part of his make-up, important in his work, but he
would never put himself in a situation where he could be
blackmailed either by members of his own cabinet, his friends
or enemies here [in Ireland] or by the British ... Mick was
always yards ahead in his planning ... He liked Hazel, every-
134

body did, you couldn't but! That was all there was to it! As I told you she was different, upper-class, very dramatic. Mick told me she liked to feel accepted by the Irish, and was glad to be useful.'[17]

Ulick O'Connor has written that Oliver St John Gogarty told him that Hazel 'could make a funeral feast entertaining. She was always thinking about other people and she had an absolute genius for tact'.[18] Oliver Gogarty himself wrote that she wanted to share in Collins' 'dangers' and responsibilities and was therefore 'willing to be identified with him in every way'.

Hazel wrote sympathetically to Michael: 'Meanwhile all our thoughts and prayers are with you, Michael. I purchased a most expensive and gigantic candle on Sunday at early Mass and burnt it for your victory. God bless you, H.' Another fragment of an undated letter said to have been found on Collins' body after he was killed reads: 'How fine and impressive and marvellously organised it all is – I am so *so* proud, Michael how can I say it all! "at all", your letter has just come to me forwarded from London, may God keep you – Hazel.'[19]

Hazel continued to be a guest in the home of Conservative MP Philip Sassoon, a lavish political host. There she often met his friend, Lloyd George. It was into Sassoon's room that the Irish delegation had been shown on their arrival in London.[20]

Mick wrote to Kitty on 12 December: 'Am back but I'm so tired that I can scarcely remain awake. This is a line to tell you so, and to say I am thinking very very much of you today, also to say that, no matter how short my note is, I am writing it.'

The 'short note' was to be the pattern of many of his letters, but he continued to write, no matter what demands were on him. He would enquire about her health, and she about his – if one of them had a cold this would be mentioned in the next letter. Both of them lit candles for each other.

Though extremely busy Mick tried to get down to Granard as often as possible, or failing that, to send Kitty a telegram to come to Dublin.

The Sunday after the turbulent cabinet meeting he was in Granard, but extremely tired. 'I was sorry you felt so tired. I just got panicky before you left at how awful you were looking and all you had to face. So I pray you may have a rest and a sleep,' Kitty wrote. The love between them was growing stronger. 'It was lovely to see you, only you were so tired and longed to sleep. It was I kept you up in a kind of way. I mean if I ran away to bed, you might have gone – and I was sorry. But that's always the way with you and I, we never want to separate. I hope it will always be that way. But it will, won't it?' Kitty pleaded.

His hurried note brought her great comfort. 'You feel very sure now,' she responded. 'Sure you might guess before you came on Sunday that I would think like you, and your worry be my worry.' His worries were great at this moment, and she understood, 'I just want to tell you that I'll be praying for you that you do and say the thing that's best for Ireland.'[21]

He received this letter on the morning of 14 December, when the Dáil debate on the Treaty was about to begin. He wrote her a short note: 'Am trying to show you that you are in my personal mind notwithstanding all cares and worries. I have so many. Do keep on praying for me.'

His hope was that the problems of the country would be sorted out shortly. 'Then,' he wrote, 'we can see how the future goes. It's all a dreadful strain and it's telling a good deal on me, but with God's help, things will be all right and some good will have been done.'[22]

TURMOIL IN THE DÁIL

On the morning of 14 December 1921 in the National University building, Earlsfort Terrace, Dublin, the Dáil debate on the Treaty began.

In many of the speeches Collins was the main target of the anti-Treaty group. The women were all anti-Treaty. In Mary MacSwiney's three hour speech which J. J. (Sceilg) O'Kelly felt was 'in the highest ranks of the greatest orators of our race,' she pointed out ominously that the issue would be either rejection by all or civil war.

Collins' forecast was proving true: 'Whatever we take back, it will be condemned'.

It was the oath which formed the greatest stumbling block and the issue of partition faded into insignificance. It was a sad, sorry spectacle – men who wanted the best for their country now spitting out venom because of it. Collins listened to the expressions of hatred and bitterness from Brugha. The bitterness was all there but it was open. Because it was honest Collins would never hold it against Brugha.

During the intervals Collins could be seen striding up and down the corridors of the National University, alone. He wore a moody and defiant look.

During these past five days Mick's letters to Kitty reflected his inner turmoil: 'Am up early this morning, and am not feeling well at all unfortunately. The times are getting worse indeed and these coming days will be worse still'.[1] And a few days later: 'I do feel so neglectful – yet you understand now, don't you, dear Kit? ... – that I have you before my mind in spite of everything and you will be there always'.[2] Then a few lines 'very late' that Saturday night: 'still at Dáil meeting and very worn out indeed. But am thinking of you,' he wrote. The next morning he wrote again during 'a temporary cessation'. He noted: 'All this business is very, very sad. Harry [Boland] has come out strongly against us. I'm sorry for that, but I suppose that like many another episode in this business must be borne also. I haven't an idea of how it will all end but, with God's help, all right. In any event I shall be satisfied'.[3]

Harry Boland had been sent by de Valera to America 'to prepare the American people for the acceptance of something short of a Republic'. When he heard the Agreement had been signed on 6 December, he made a public pronouncement welcoming it. But when he learned of de Valera's opposition he cabled to the Dáil his wish to have it on record that he would vote as de Valera would, against the Treaty. Now, Harry was Mick's opponent in politics just as he had been his rival for Kitty, the love of his life.

Kitty wrote to him commenting on those who were for him and against him. 'The papers to-day are interesting enough. It is nothing but Collins here, Collins all the time, and as far as I can gather from strangers coming here, it's the same all over Ireland.'[4] She was concerned about his health, and wanted to be with him – to talk – writing was no substitute. 'I am very lonely at the thought of not seeing you this week-end; in fact I am very lonely just now,' she wrote. 'You must be having an anxious time, but don't worry, all will yet be well, and it won't be your fault if the country is brought into trouble again.'[5]

On 19 December the Dáil reassembled in public session. It was a day of speeches full of emotion and bitterness. Griffith rose to propose formally that the Treaty be approved. After de Valera spoke against the Treaty, Collins made a passionate speech in its favour: 'In my opinion it gives us freedom, not the ultimate freedom that all nations desire and develop to, but the freedom to achieve it'.

Next morning as he had done every morning, he went to Mass. On 20 December he wrote to Kitty:

Yesterday was the worst day I ever spent in my life but thanks be to God it's over. The Treaty will almost certainly be beaten and then no one knows what will happen. The country is certainly quite clearly for it but that seems to be little good, as their voices are not heard ... [6]

As one day moved into the next, the debate continued with undiminished bitterness. 'It is not hard to know how all my thoughts are fully occupied in this momentous hour,' he told Kitty.

On 22 December a debate on whether or not there should be adjournment for Christmas brought out some of the most venomous words. That evening Kathleen Clarke came to him. She had spoken against the agreement and wanted to explain that if her husband were alive he would not have voted for it. 'I wouldn't want you to vote for it. All I ask is that, if it's passed, you give us the chance to work it,' was Collins' response.[7] Later Barton and Mick spoke for the last time. Mick replied to a remark of Barton's that he was honouring his signature: 'We all signed under the duress of our own conscience.'

The following morning he wrote a hurried note to Kitty saying that the previous day 'came so strenuous' that he was unable to finish the note he started writing to her.

Finally, on 23 December the Dáil agreed that the house would recess and reassemble on 3 January 1922. Unfortunately attitudes, far from mellowing in the interim, became more entrenched. Mick was sad. A friend noted, 'all the fun had gone out of him.' Over the festive period he would have to meet many a former friend, uncertain of their feelings towards him. But this was a price he was prepared to pay. He was going home to west Cork for Christmas. He would go to Kitty in Granard for the New Year.

Down in Woodfield and Sam's Cross he found the usual welcome. But there was much discussion, and many of the debates on Ireland's future were subdued. Most of the neighbours and his old friends would stand by him. But one great friend, Tom Hales, who had finally been released from Pentonville Prison, would not agree. He had suffered too much to give in now. If war was the alternative to total freedom and allegiance to Ireland, then war it would be. Mick said afterwards, 'More than any man I would have valued his support'. However, Tom's brother, Seán, who had been in Frongoch with Mick, would in the end stand by him. That division in the family, repeated numerous times throughout the country, was a symbol of a divided people. But for the present, this Christmas of 1921, all would be friends. Mick would put aside his doubts, his worries, his anxieties and would enjoy Christmas at home – a Christmas not 'on the run'.

A reinvigorated Mick returned to Dublin just after Christmas, but it was straight to work. On 28 December, he wrote to Kitty 'a line before a meeting starts. Am looking forward to a very strenuous day as we are working hard for the resumption after Xmas'. There was a number of meetings to try and reach a consensus prior to the Dáil assembly. The Labour Party had proposed a way to avoid a division in the Dáil, but he had become apprehensive. He visited his sister Katie, who was in a Dublin hospital. 'I've strained every nerve to get support for the Treaty,' he told her, 'but I'm hoping now we'll be defeated at the division.'

Puzzled, she asked him why.

'Either way there's going to be trouble,' was his response. Despite the disadvantages of now being known, he would choose to face the British military machine rather than to face a fight against his own countrymen. 'I would rather see it thrown out than passed by a very narrow majority,' he told a friend.[8]

Mick went down to Granard for New Year's Day. It was a happy time. He and Kitty seriously discussed their future and plans for marriage as soon as the political turmoil settled.

140

In a short note on the morning of 3 January prior to the reassembly of the Dáil he told Kitty, 'I am so happy about it all, much much more happy as I think more and more of it all'. At least something was going right for him; their relationship was on an even keel; he had found true love.[9]

Treaty Divides Friends

When the Dáil reassembled on 3 January 1922 Collins began the day with a suggestion that they should accept the Treaty without a division and authorise the foundation of a Provisional Government. 'If necessary,' he said to the anti-Treaty group, 'you can fight the Provisional Government on the Republican question afterwards.'

'We will do that if you carry ratification, perhaps,' responded de Valera scornfully.

'Believe me,' said Collins, 'the Treaty gives us the one opportunity we may ever get in our history for going forward to our idea of a free and independent Ireland. This cannot be gained without very much work yet – very hard work and perhaps more hard work ... It is not by denial of liberty that we can reach liberty.'

Countess Markievicz at one point stung Collins by repeating the rumour in circulation that as 'Princess Mary's wedding is to be broken off ... the Princess Mary is to be married to Michael Collins who will be appointed First Governor'. This hit a nerve. Collins rose and said:

> ... it is an insult to my name and to the name of a lady belonging to a foreign nation that I cannot allow to pass. Some time in our history as a nation a girl went through Ireland and was not insulted by the people of Ireland [this is a reference to an earlier comment on the activities of Constance Markievicz]. I do not come from the class that the deputy for the Dublin division comes from; I come from the plain people of Ireland. The lady whose name was mentioned is, I understand, betrothed to some man. I know nothing of her personally, but the statement may cause her pain, and may cause pain to the lady who is betrothed to me. I just stand in that plain way, and I will not allow without challenge any deputy in the assembly of my nation to insult any lady either of this nation or of any other nation.

Mick wanted Kitty to have the right version of the story before she heard it or perhaps read it in the paper, so he sent her a telegram that evening: 'My dear, dear Kitty, see the reference to yourself and princess Mary of England. My Betrothed, My fondest love.'[1]

There were meetings at night to try to find a compromise, but no compromise could be found; the long-drawn-out debate continued. Collins had pointed out that the Articles of Agreement were not a Treaty as such, that the Dáil had to ratify them and the signatories were only recommending the document for acceptance.

What with wrangling over procedures and amendments and policy differences and some bitter invective, 5 January was a gruelling day. That night, very very late, Mick sat down to write 'just one or two lines' to Kitty. 'This is the worst day I have had yet – far far the worst. May God help us all ... In awful haste.' Here was his deep inner feeling – a cry for an exit!

Earlier that night he had met Harry Boland, who was back from America. He tried to persuade him to change his mind, but failed. 'He was friendly, of course, and very nice,' Mick told Kitty. However, next day, Mick recorded, 'I'm afraid though he was not so nice today but not about you – I mean not on the subject of you [Kitty]. I'm afraid he wasn't fair in his homecoming in what he said about our [Treaty] side today. He's working like the very devil against us, but God is good'.[2]

It was 8.30 on the evening of 7 January when Arthur Griffith finished speaking. Then de Valera with a few brief words asked the house to reject the Treaty in favour of Document No. 2. Collins concluded: 'Let the Irish nation judge us now and for future years'.

The time to vote had arrived. The Treaty was approved by a majority of seven.

There was no exultation. Collins was on his feet to seize the moment. 'It is no victory,' he said as he called for unity.

'I make the promise publicly to the Irish nation that I will do my best, and, though some people here have said hard things of me, I would not stand things like that said about the other side. I have just as high a regard for some of them, and am prepared to do as much for them now, as always. The President knows how I tried to do my best for him.'

'Hear, hear!' de Valera interrupted.

Collins stretched out his hand towards him, stating, 'Well, he has exactly the same position in my heart now as he always had'. De Valera seemed pleased but before he could respond, Mary MacSwiney rose, said she rejected any proposals and called the vote 'the grossest act of betrayal that Ireland has ever endured'.

The dream of unity was shattered. Many wept in despair at this moment. Enduring friendships were now truly split.

Outside the Dáil, crowds cheered when news of the decision on the vote filtered through.

On 9 January 1922 the Dáil reassembled. Amid scenes of chaos, de Valera resigned as president of the Dáil.

After a weary day Mick wrote 'in awful haste' to Kitty: 'I'm absolutely fagged out and worn out and everything ... If you knew how the other side is "killing" me – God help me. We had to beat them again today'.[3]

Next day, he wrote to Kitty he was 'running back to the University for more talk – talk – talk. How I wish I could see you for a few minutes and if you only realised how I have missed hearing from you ... please do write. You can scarcely realise how I wish for you ... Your very own all right now!'[4]

On the following day de Valera and his supporters left the Dáil in protest, Arthur Griffith was then elected president of Dáil Éireann (Second Dáil). He appointed his cabinet, among them Michael Collins as minister of finance.

Later that night Mick reflected: 'The whole business was awful and I feel exactly like you about it,' responding to

Kitty's 'wish it was over' sigh. He knew she would see it in the papers. Right now 'I am wishing to God I could be with you and had left it all. The tactics of the opposition were not very creditable at times ... '[5]

Only pro-Treaty deputies attended a meeting on 14 January 1922 to formally ratify the Treaty and to select a Provisional Government to run until 6 December 1922, unless the people should reject it at the polls. Michael Collins was elected chairman; Griffith had no post in this Provisional Government.

(At this time there were – in coexistence – Dáil Éireann with Griffith as president with a cabinet, and the Provisional Government with Collins as chairman. Some ministers held posts both in the Dáil cabinet and in the Provisional Government.)

One of the proudest moments for Mick Collins was on the morning of 16 January 1922, when he took over Dublin Castle from the British, the seat of British administration and its military headquarters in Ireland for over seven centuries. Mick had been down in Granard with Kitty for the weekend and due to a train strike he was twenty minutes late for the historic ceremony. As he awaited the start of a Provisional Government meeting, he penned a few lines to Kitty wanting to share the moment with her:

> I am as happy a man as there is in Ireland today ... Have just taken over Dublin Castle ... Otherwise I see all sorts of difficulties ahead, but never mind ... There is nobody like you, I find, and I wish I'd been nicer to you.[6]

With no other social outlet, and few whom he could trust, he began to rely on Kitty. He took full responsibility for any misunderstanding there had been between them –' 'Twas my fault,' he wrote.

He disliked getting the better of his friend Harry Boland in love – politics was another matter. He told Kitty that he 'just said to him [Harry] that he had little chance in that quarter now'.[7] Harry accepted it with good grace and wrote to Kitty: 'I want to congratulate you. M [Mick] told me of your engagement, and I wish you long life and happiness. – Ever yours, H. Boland'.[8]

So the love triangle was now sorted out.

Mick felt that at present there was much to be done for the country and he was in a hurry. He set up temporary headquarters of the Provisional Government in City Hall, then moved to a building in Merrion Street beside where Griffith had established Dáil Éireann headquarters. Collins was an important link between the two governments, which functioned in parallel. (Cosgrave, Duggan and Kevin O'Higgins were members of both ministries.)

The division in the cabinet was repeated in the Army Council. At the February Cumann na mBan Convention, Mary MacSwiney spoke against the Treaty. She said the 'women were the backbone of the nation,' and she urged her peers to reaffirm their allegiance to the Republic. Jennie Wyse-Power, however, agreed with Michael Collins that 'it seemed easier to get the Republic from a government working in Ireland by Irishmen than from an Ireland under British rule'.[9] Cumann na mBan rejected the Treaty, so a woman's organisation in support of the Treaty took the name of Cumann na Saoirse (Society of Freedom).

Collins, in a difficult situation as president of the militant IRB and its most dominant figure, sought to maintain unity in the hope that the constitution which was in preparation would help to satisfy the more extreme elements.

Problems were mounting, with the IRA splintered and evacuated army barracks throughout the country being taken over, in some places, by pro-Treaty and in others by anti-Treaty military personnel. At first there was sporadic unrest, intimidation and coercion but gradually and with increasing militancy the floodgates opened.

146

The country had begun to split and Mick Collins hated this. Mick knew that men like Brugha and Stack were motivated partly by old jealousy and resentment but now in a surprise move, Rory O'Connor, a friend of Mick's and member of GHQ, began to organise opposition to the Treaty.

Mick could see conflict looming when the IRA demanded that a convention should be held. He was torn between political demands and military claims. On 20 January he had to go to London to meet Sir James Craig, the northern prime minister. Already trouble had flared up in the north – talk of a Boundary Commission and the release of internees had caused Unionists to react violently. They attacked Catholic areas in Belfast; thirty people were killed in one night, and a stream of refugees was driven across the border.

Kitty came to 'Dunleary' (Mick's spelling) on 20 January to see him off on the mailboat. As he journeyed on the rough sea to his destination he wrote her a few lines on how 'very vividly' she was in his thoughts – 'May it be always like this and any time we leave each other ... I'll say a small prayer for you'. He had only two hours' sleep in the Jermyn Court Hotel, then at 8.30 he went to the Laverys' to speak to Sir John about the Sir Hugh Lane pictures. (Lady Gregory had written to Collins on 14 January 1922 about this collection coming to Ireland rather than staying in England – 'Sir John Lavery says you are the man whose request will carry most weight with the London Government,' she wrote.) Despite his heavy schedule and his many problems he broached the subject with advisers of the British government. He got a mixed reaction, but he promised Lady Gregory that he would pursue the matter.[10]

There was a four-hour meeting of the Irish group with Craig concerning the boycott of Belfast goods. They reached 'an agreement' of which Mick told Kitty in his few brief lines on 21 January, with his 'fondest love'.[11] Mick's dislike for politicians comes through in a letter to his friend John

O'Kane that night: 'They will have me for what I am not. The more the rigmarole of my life continues to encompass politics the more uneasy I feel. I am a soldier ... '[12]

That night Hazel and John Lavery entertained both the British group and the Irish delegation which included Collins, Duggan and Kevin O'Higgins. Lady Juliet Duff who was there commented that: 'three nicer men she'd never met,' and found Collins 'quite irresistible ... with a tremendous twinkle and sudden quick impulsive gestures'.[13]

Collins was back in Dublin on 22 January and on 23 January he had a note delivered to Kitty, who was in town. He asked if he could meet her at 2 o'clock: 'Will you come to the Dolphin [Hotel] and I'll wait for you at the door, or will you say any better place where I can pick you up and bring you there?'

A week later he again met Craig in Dublin. Feelings ran high when Craig made it clear that the north-east would not be part of the 'new state'. Furthermore, a threat that some Volunteers who had been captured in the north could be hanged had Collins mentioning the subject of reprisals. He ignored the activities of MacEoin, Aiken and others who had carried out a series of raids in the north in retaliation for the killings of Catholics which had become a nightly occurrence in the north.

According to the Craig-Collins agreement the Dáil cabinet on 24 January agreed to lift the boycott on Belfast goods. Immediately trade was resumed and some Catholic workers who had been dismissed from the shipyards were reinstated. However, conflict continued. A further meeting between the two men broke up in February. Up to March, Collins and Craig met a few times, but promises had little effect and violence in the north-east against nationalists continued unabated. Craig did not help the situation when he publicly reinforced the north's separate identity under the Government of Ireland Act.

148

As well as the northern problem, Mick was trying to administer law and order in the rest of the country, and handling the transition from the British administration. More than anything he was personally distressed by the thought of the disloyalty of former comrades.

A friend wrote from America and appealed to him not to break with de Valera and Harry Boland. Collins in his reply regretted that both men were 'on the other side' because, he wrote: 'We are going forward ... surely no one will claim that we can possibly be worse off ...' Speaking of Harry Boland he said: '... there is no need for me to tell you what I have thought of him in the past, and I need only to say that my feelings towards both the President and himself are still as cordial as they were'.[14]

The taking over of army barracks countrywide continued, in some cases with violence between local IRA pro- and anti-Treaty factions. In Dublin pro-Treaty authorities ensured that evacuated barracks would remain loyal to whatever government would be elected, and Beggars Bush Barracks became headquarters of what was to become the uniformed National Army.

By 29 January 1922, Collins expressed his disappointment to Kitty at the anti-Treaty stance of Sinn Féin clubs: 'Tralee after the Auxies had gone, Galway the same. God help us from them. They're beauties.'[15]

He retained the loyalty of the Squad, as well as the majority of GHQ; but he bitterly regretted that in his own county of Cork, friends and colleagues such as Liam Deasy, Tom Barry, Liam Lynch, Seán Hyde, and his great friend Tom Hales opposed his views. Cathal Brugha and Liam Mellows, in keeping with their strong convictions, had begun to tour Ireland to meet Volunteer commands where they pledged them 'to maintain the existing Republic'. They were sowing the seeds of revolt among impressionable young men.

Mick wrote to Kitty: 'I am really and truly having an awful

time and am rapidly becoming quite desperate. Oh Lord, it's honestly frightful'.[16]

Love, Turmoil, Crowded Schedule

Since their official engagement at Christmas 1921, Mick had grown in his love for Kitty. He had given her an engagement ring, which she would sometimes call 'a representative', at other times 'a reminder' of him. Though circumstances prevented them from being together as often as they would have liked, they communicated their deep affection for one another in their letters. Mick's letters, though more discreet and subdued than Kitty's, nevertheless reveal his tender affection for her, his concern for her well-being and his anticipation of her becoming his wife.

He seldom omitted to tell her how much he looked forward to her letters, as she did to his, and he let her know that his family approved of her. 'Mary is in love with you,' he wrote of his sister.

Constantly they were in each other's prayers. 'Was at a Requiem Mass for the Holy Father today. Said a full rosary for you alone,' he wrote on 31 January 1922.

'Badgered all day since my return [from Granard] and am off to a meeting now,' Mick wrote to Kitty on 3 February.

Despite the split on the Treaty Collins was careful to allow continued support money for Sinéad de Valera and her family. On 3 February she returned to him a cheque for £50 because, she wrote, 'Éamon is no longer President since last month'. She signed the letter, 'Your friend always'.

The next day the northern problem again hit him; he had a sudden call to London. In a note to Kitty he wrote, 'The Craig business is serious, and if we don't find some way of dealing with it, all the bravos [Dublinites] will get a great chance of distinguishing themselves once more ... I wish you were coming to London with me tonight ... Must do a million things by 7 o'clock,' he wrote 'in haste'.

Next morning, an early breakfast in foggy London, 'then

Mass, then conferences for the whole day'.[1] These meetings accomplished little. 'Things do not appear to be very promising,' he told Kitty, but added, 'perhaps it's a question of being 'the darkest hour before the dawn ... With fondest love.'[2]

Though there was some agreement, and Collins and the group returned to Ireland that night, the situation on the ground in the north-east deteriorated.

On 9 February Mick told Kitty he'd most likely get down on Saturday. 'Honestly, Kit, you don't know the rush. It's awful. It was a good job you did not ask me if I enjoyed my time in London. It was heartbreaking simply. Fighting the English there. Fighting our own people here. It's the very frozen limit.'

On 10 February 1922, he had planned to visit her at the weekend. He had withdrawn sixty pounds to buy her a gold watch. Beforehand he wrote:

> ... – please dear dear Kit. When I meet you – and this much I'll ask also – you'll have to give me a couple of hours in the morning for work. Otherwise you'll have all my time ... Several people clamouring for me. Do forgive this scraggy note. You don't know how anxious I am to see you. I have a kind of feeling that I must go away with you – strain telling on me also. May God be with you.

Kitty's 'fairy-like' beauty was commented on by an ex-serviceman, Major Harris, who saw her at the hunt dance and at private dances in Westmeath; afterwards he wrote that 'one of the prettiest pictures in the *Express* has been that of Miss Kitty Kiernan, the intended bride of the Financial Minister of the Irish Free State ... whose presence would grace the life of any man however highly placed, and whose inborn native beauty is portrayed in every outline of her life.'[3]

But for Mick there was more to a woman than beauty. Being an avid reader himself, he introduced Kitty to Edward Fitzgerald's translation of Omar Khayyam's *The Rubaiyat* – he wanted it to be a topic of conversation at their next meeting.[4]

By mid-February they were discussing a house in Greystones which he had set his sights on. He asked her to be patient and understanding of him, he doesn't mind being 'lectured to ... do not think too badly of me for all my headstrong ways and my bad temper, and my impatience at being given good advice'.[5] He had spent a day sick in bed. In her 'good advice' Kitty tells him to take life a little easier: 'I don't consider that you will really do Ireland or the people of Ireland any good by killing yourself working ... You are the one that, by living for Ireland, helps her'.[6]

Just as he got her letter he was 'rushing off to a meeting in the Mansion House' but as it could last longer than anticipated, he wrote, 'I am not chancing leaving writing you until afterwards'.[7]

Kitty had hesitated during the weekend when Mick had 'suggested' a June wedding, so she said, 'I went to chapel to-night to pray for you, and during that time thought that making the little sacrifices are no use if I couldn't make the big one, and it's June D.V. Now I don't mean it's really a sacrifice in that sense, but just putting it off until I'd be ready ... And so now I have proposed to you! Are you satisfied?' She agreed she could take care of him and he would be all the better for it if they were married.[8]

Collins agreed with de Valera to postpone elections for three months. Meanwhile the country became increasingly anarchic, although bloodshed was for the time being avoided.

By mid-March Kitty had become of interest to photojournalists. They descended on Granard, and pictures of her in her 'black evening dress' were published widely. In the *Sketch* of 8 March, there are three photographs of 'M. Collins' fiancée, Miss Kitty Kiernan' with Sir John Lavery's portrait of Collins on the opposite page. Kitty resented some of the write-ups about herself and asked Michael 'to compose a little piece. I will take an action against them if they continue to publish the rot they [*The Irish Record*] are writing,' Kitty had written on 14 February. She resented the linking of herself and Lady Lavery in Michael's affections.[9]

There were times when Mick expressed his affection for Kitty very strongly – 'I want to see you and that's that. I do want to see you – Kitty Kiernan. I do badly. Just away from Sinn Féin Ard-Fheis for an hour's interval'. His love for her had to be slotted in between the multitude of political and military demands on him. 'Isn't it nice to think of you in every free moment – oh! and in moments that are not free too? God be with you, my dear, dear Kitty.'[10]

She had written to him about a problem she had had in finding one of her silk stockings. He responded: 'I'd love to have seen you wandering around looking for a stocking – a single silk stocking'. In that letter of 10 March he told her, 'I said a whole rosary for you last night'.[11]

While Mick went about his gruelling task of countrywide pro-Treaty campaigning, liaising with various groups and endless meetings, Kitty was often off to a dance: 'going to dance in the Gresham 17th [March]'. She had a dancing partner to take her 'all to myself' she wrote. 'I suppose there will be talk of my dancing with him a lot but, when *you* don't object, I hope they talk about something new for a change. I may see Harry too, but trust me.'

As Mick was about to travel to Cork to do his duty for Ireland, 'my duty' she wrote, would be 'to go and have a good time. And yet we have a grand feeling that we can trust each other, knowing that if either of us offends we will pay the penalty sooner or later in remorse ... By Saturday evening when you come back I'll be tired of everybody, and then will have *you* to amuse me'.[12]

Meanwhile, Mick was asking her, 'When are you coming up to town again? It is years and years since I saw you although indeed you are before my mind every bit as much as you could wish ... Am looking forward to seeing you'.[13]

154

Collins was enthusiastically cheered when he addressed a crowd on the Treaty issue in Cork City early in March. A Mrs Agnellis in the crowd that night observed that: 'He was at one and the same time the youthful dashing leader we had learned to love and admire; and yet a figure on which strain, worry, and overwork had taken its toll'.

Momentarily he paused. Mrs Agnellis, who stood quite close, called to him, 'God bless you, Michael Collins!'

He looked down from the platform and said clearly, 'I need it!'[14]

Later that night as he and Seán MacEoin made their way to the house of his sister, Mary Collins-Powell, he narrowly missed being shot by a lone gunman.

As Mick's schedule became more crowded he found it 'difficult to write a real letter.' On 24 March he sent her 'a little note ... I am looking forward to seeing you in fifteen minutes. So goodbye until then. All my love. Mícheál'.

On 28 March in a note to Kitty he wrote, 'I'm sorry I'm looking old! Am I really? And not so fresh? If you saw the way I've had to write this letter – about a thousand interruptions.' He was to go to Bangor for a meeting with Craig and intended calling on her on the way back but he got a wire to go to London instead. 'Saw Harry today – he'll be with you I think on Thursday.' He wasn't worried about Harry because he knew that Kitty had now given her love to him.[15]

Discussions were difficult. 'These two days have been the worse [sic] days I have ever spent. The representatives from the North are very very difficult – they are in a way more difficult than the others, but even so one always hopes.' And next day: 'Have had the devil's own day between the North and the English. Things are pretty serious, but there is always hope, so *that's that*. How are you? I wish you were here – am going to the Laverys to dinner this evening, so that means that we'll be back [home] early.'[16]

Collins travelled a great deal to drum up support for the

Treaty. He was in London on 30 March in an effort to solve the tensions in Northern Ireland which had been caused by rioting, burning of Catholic homes and conflicts with the B-Specials. In a three-pronged approach, delegates from the Provisional, Northern and British governments signed an agreement of cooperation and peace between the now separate parts of Ireland.

At the conference he met Lord Londonderry for the first time. Londonderry afterwards wrote: 'I can say at once that I spent three of the most delightful hours that I ever spent in my life and I formed a conclusion of the character of Michael Collins which was quite different from the one which I would have formed if I had only known him as I had read of him before this particular interview.'[17]

In a letter on 31 March, Mick apologised for inflicting his problems on Kitty and told her he was 'sanguine about the future ... We came to an agreement ... with Craig yesterday,' regarding the release of prisoners. 'But the news from Ireland is very bad, and the "powers that be" here are getting very alarmed and there may be a bust-up at any moment' – a reference to Rory O'Connor and anti-Treaty activities.[18]

On and off Kitty's health was not good and by the end of March she was told by the doctor that she would have to take it easy for two months. Mick insisted that she should carry out the doctor's wishes and have a quiet holiday somewhere. On his return journey from Castlebar in early April he detoured to Granard, but 'was not pleased' with her appearance so he insisted that a quiet holiday was essential for her. He said he had assembled a parcel of books and would send them direct to wherever she chose.

Harry Boland was still friendly with Kitty and he would often visit Granard for a day at the hunt. While Michael was writing that 'things are rapidly becoming as bad as they can be, and the country has before it what may be the worst period yet,' Kitty was replying about 'going to Longford races'.[19]

In mid-April, when Kitty chastised Michael for not writing to her often, he appealed to her for understanding.

> If you could only see the circumstances under which most of them [the letters] are written, you wouldn't be so mighty quick to disparage them. At any rate I won't mind you this time ... We did nothing at the Conference yesterday – except talk, talk all the time – it's simply awful. And the country! But they never think of the country at all – they only think of finding favour for their own theories, they only think of getting their own particular little scheme accepted.

In a postscript he noted, 'The Rebel Army has taken over the Four Courts. God help them!'[20]

Rory O'Connor, on behalf of the anti-Treatyite Executive Army Council which had split from GHQ, with Liam Mellows and other anti-Treaty leaders had seized the Four Courts in Dublin as headquarters. They fortified the building on the night of the 13–14 April. Liam Lynch, the chief of staff, did not share O'Connor's views; like Liam Deasy, commander of the First Southern Division, he was anxious to give civil administration a further chance. Michael Collins was reluctant to push O'Connor, Mellows and his followers – all former friends and colleagues – from the Four Courts.

'It's simply awful,' he wrote to Kitty, as he appealed for understanding for not visiting her. 'They [the Republican Executive] never think of the country at all – they only think of finding favour for their own theories ... this Rebel Army.'[21]

On 16 April, Collins narrowly missed being shot in Dublin. This attack received widespread publicity. Kitty worried when she read of it and sent him a telegram, but he was quick to reassure her, 'You knew I'd be all right, didn't you?' Ever the optimist, 'God is better to us than we deserve ... Honestly I did not know that I was going to Naas ... It was immediately after our return the shooting took place. I think they must have meant to capture me only. They were

157

great optimists. God help them, but they are carrying things a bit too far'.[22]

Since the beginning of April, seizures of cars, lorries, and attacks on pro-Treaty troops had become a regular occurrence. There were attempts at negotiation but these kept breaking down. While Churchill regarded Rory O'Connor and his men as mutineers and wanted either to 'starve them out' or use militant action against them, Collins saw them as Irishmen and former colleagues.[23] He would not be pushed into reacting hastily. Moreover, he still viewed them as important allies needed to support fellow nationalists in the north.

When it became clear to the IRA that it was unlikely that any worthwhile gains would result from the Craig-Collins agreement, they stepped up plans for a northern offensive. Already Volunteer units had positioned themselves in the north, where they were in receipt of arms derived from two shipments.

Despite the division in the army and in political circles, Michael Collins agreed with Liam Lynch to the dispatch by secret means to the north of a large consignment of these arms to help northern Catholics, many of whom were the victims of sectarian killings. Cosgrave, Blythe and cabinet members were aware of the transaction.[24]

Though Collins was playing with fire and risking the British reoccupation of the entire country, it was a gamble he was willing to take. To him this ambivalence was preferable to outright civil war.[25] Because retaliations grew more severe on Catholics after IRA raids and also because Craig was using the raids as an excuse for sectarian violence, it was decided to call off the northern offensive.

Collins continued to be reluctant to act against former comrades in the Four Courts, although it was becoming obvious that despite his best efforts the deteriorating situation was leading towards civil war. As meetings continued, he clung to the hope of halting all-out confrontation and, contrary to the wishes of Griffith and other cabinet members, decided to enter an agreement with de Valera, which became known as The Pact. This provided for a coalition panel in a national government where the anti-Treaty party would be represented in the cabinet in the ratio of four to five.

Collins argued, 'It was a last effort on our part to avoid strife, to prevent the use of force by Irishmen against Irishmen'.[26]

The Pact gave Collins a brief respite. There would be some evening time to visit old friends. While on the run he had often used Dr Oliver St John Gogarty's house in Ely Place. He would renew his friendship with this medical doctor who had on many an occasion 'operated on wounded volunteers'.[27]

He would also have more time for Kitty, who was ill. Her health had not been strong since the previous summer.

Since the beginning of May she had been spending some time resting in the Grand Hotel, Greystones; here Mick would call for a brief chat late in the evenings, whenever time allowed. They would talk and talk, both agreed on the value of the 'long chats'.

The respite was short-lived. Soon Michael Collins was again summoned to London.

Kitty's demands and the lack of understanding she sometimes displayed in her letters put even more pressure on Mick. Though she was well aware how difficult it was for him, she was, in her impatient way, hoping he could put a speedy end to the conflict and meetings. 'I had a list of your meetings in my mind from the night I last left Dublin,' she wrote. 'Oh no, I'd never invite you to Granard on the eve of a big meeting so far away as Tralee where you must go the day before ... what fools Irishmen are to give up everything for their country.'[28]

He had to write, 'Sorry I can't possibly leave town owing to the situation here'. But, 'I am very anxious to see you. It seems about a million years since we met and that's a long time ...' Two days later he would write again: 'There will be no chance that I can go down tomorrow night as I have to leave on the morning train on Saturday for Tralee and Killarney. Then I won't be back until Monday evening. I've had every Sunday at it now since the Dublin meeting, and it's becoming wearying, but maybe we'll have a rest soon'.[29]

By the end of April the name of Michael Collins could be found on morning papers not alone in Ireland but in England and America. In order to secure support for the Treaty and avoid civil war, it became necessary for him to increase his number of appearances at public meetings. This caused Kitty great anxiety; because of his long hours of standing on cold, windswept platforms he constantly suffered from colds. She repeatedly pressed him to get more sleep – she had noticed that on visits to Granard he would sometimes fall asleep, depriving her of his company. 'I saw the *Sunday Independent* ... about Saturday's meeting [in Cork],' she wrote on 25 April. 'So I was "wondering" how you would do on Sunday or would yourself and Seán be shot!' By return he reassured her in a note sent via Gearóid O'Sullivan that he was well but lonely for her.

Her own health was far from good and some of her letters and his refer to this. However, by May she would be in Greystones taking that long-needed health rest. She would also be closer to her lover, who would visit her in the late evenings. Both of them longed for a normal life.

Partly from a habit of caution and partly because of lack of time, Mick rarely dealt with political issues in any depth when writing to Kitty but they discussed politics and problems when they met. He knew that she and her brother Larry still received visits from Harry Boland and he did not want to place her in a difficult situation. Kitty made reference to Harry in one of her letters: ' ... if he is not to be trusted', she wrote, 'I wouldn't take much of that particular "thing" with him. Enough said! ... I want to talk to you again [about it].'[30]

160

Kitty never failed to mention any of Harry's visits to Mick; it came as no surprise when in a letter of 26 April, she noted that 'Dev is still at it. Last time H [Harry] was here he told me (in a burst of confidence) of Dev's dislike for you, because you were too anxious for power, that Dev liked Griffith, but Harry dislikes Griffith, and (of course) likes you, etc.' There was more but she would spare it for when next they would meet.[31]

'I knew that about de V. well. I have known it all along. That's what he says of everyone who opposes him. He has done it in America similarly. It's just typical of him,' Mick wrote in response to Kitty. 'I wish to God I was rid of it all and was just with you and free from their scurrilities and their accusations and counter-accusations.'[32]

In an interview with Hayden Talbot, Mick pointed out that while he himself could only take the facts as he found them, de Valera preached idealism: 'He knows ... that the Republican ideal is as dear to us who support the Treaty as it is to himself ... He knows that we who oppose him will work to make Ireland strong enough to declare her Independence ...[33]

On 27 April Mick was 'just preparing to go to a Dáil meeting, and that's a prospect that doesn't appeal to me in the least. God help us all!' he wrote to Kitty, and he told her he had been 'thinking of her all morning ... Are you not coming to town? Please do if you can at all as I want so badly to see you'.

'ENGLISH LADY' UNDER SUSPICION

The month of May was extremely difficult for Mick, and though he eventually succeeded in convincing people on both sides of the Treaty that the Pact was necessary, he had yet to convince the London government, which had already denounced it. In a letter to Churchill he explained his decision, but Churchill, being committed to the Treaty, was not convinced and summoned him to London. Armed with the draft constitution, Griffith, Duggan, Kevin O'Higgins and Hugh Kennedy went over on 25 May, and Mick was to travel next day.

But first he would attend to spiritual matters. The Reverend Frank Gibney was giving a Mission in a church in Greystones. Mick 'was very busy in Dublin, worked and worried almost beyond endurance. He got to Greystones very late and very tired. It was the eve of his departure to London re the Pact. He got up next morning as early as 5.30 a.m., came to the church and made a glorious confession.'

After confession he said to Fr Gibney, 'Father, say the Mass for Ireland!' Fr Gibney told his congregation that day: 'You saw one of Ireland's hidden saints making no small sacrifice for the Master this morning'. About 'an hour or so afterwards he crossed for London'.[1]

With time to think on the SS *Cambria* he felt 'more lonely' than ever for Kitty, as he anticipated the daunting task that lay ahead.

When Michael Collins arrived at Downing Street on the morning of 27 May, Lloyd George said the meeting would have to be postponed because Lord Birkenhead had a temperature. 'I never heard it called that before,' shouted Collins with laughter, and dashed off to see Birkenhead.

At the door, Birkenhead's butler said his lordship was unwell. Collins brushed past him into the hall and called out.

Birkenhead, on hearing Collins' voice, came to the landing in his dressing-gown with bottle in hand and called, 'Come along up, Michael!'[2] On this occasion the two men had a frank discussion.

In a long letter to Kitty from London on 28 May he thanked her for her 'wire' and poured his weary heart out:

Things are serious – far far more serious than any one at home thinks. In fact it is not too much to say that they are as serious as they were at the worst stage of the negotiations last year. And even while we are here there comes the news of two British soldiers being killed in Dublin and two ex-policemen in Boyle. Coming at such a time it is impossible to get away from the conclusion that they are done deliberately to make things more difficult for us in our task here. It is not very creditable to those who are responsible for the actions themselves but it is simply disastrous for the name of Ireland.[3]

Numerous meetings over the next few days proved very difficult for Collins and his colleagues in London. In 'a hurried line' to Kitty that night, Mick in desperation wrote: 'Things are bad beyond words, and I am almost without hope of being able to do anything of permanent use. It's really awful – to think of what I have to endure here owing to the way things are done by the opponents at home'.[4]

On 30 May when the draft constitution was discussed in London, the Irish delegation was told that if this form was persisted in, a break was inevitable as it was 'a clear breach of the Treaty'. To bring the groups together in convivial surroundings Lady Lavery held a dinner party. The 'evening passed pleasantly' with 'the two Churchills and their wives' and the Irish delegation.[5]

Mick in a few lines to Kitty wrote, 'The weather is awful here and everything is awful – I wish to God someone else was in the position and not I. *But that's that.*'[6]

Life was becoming ever more difficult and he could see no solution; he felt as trapped as a rabbit in a snare. To add to his problems, newspaper journalists observed the moves of the Irish contingent and especially the arrival of the 'notorious Michael Collins.' He wrote to Kitty about it (29 May):

> You ought to have seen some of the papers here yesterday – M. Collins in Downing St with his sweetheart. I can have all sorts of lovely libel actions.
>
> The Laverys took me there in their car. Some of the correspondents recognised my friend but the story was too good! I must bring you back some of the papers to show you. Am writing this in the midst of a very worrying time. But I mustn't make you worry. I wish you were here.[7]

Leon Ó Broin notes: 'The Laverys had been photographed driving Collins to Downing Street. Some newspapers "played up" the picture of Collins with "his sweetheart". The lady with Sir John was, however, Sir John's wife Hazel'.[8]

Kitty, in a postscript to her letter of 30 May, wrote: 'Don't forget to keep papers about your sweetheart! It was extraordinary, wasn't it? I'd like to see the papers. So don't forget'.

Kitty knew of the value of Lady Lavery in Mick's intelligence world. On 3 June, as well as sending her love, Kitty reminded him to bring the papers with him to Granard, 'if you have them'.

His friend Lady Hazel Lavery would from now on be publicly linked romantically to him. She did nothing to dispel the rumour – in fact she encouraged it – and it was known within her intimate circle that she was attracted to Michael Collins. There has recently been some debate about the degree of romantic involvement between Collins and Lady Lavery and how much of it was the invention of Lady Lavery. A 'fantasist' was how Oliver Gogarty described her.[9] Terence de Vere White in his biography of Kevin O'Higgins takes the same view of her.

After Collins' death she showed Birkenhead letters that

she said she had received from Michael, 'and he noticed that the occasional romantic passages were interpolated in a woman's handwriting valiantly, if unsuccessfully, disguised.' It was, said Terence de Vere White, 'all very odd, very unreal but not unpleasant, when one became accustomed to it and accepted the romantic convention'.[10]

Her husband accepted her lively imagination, and the 'imaginary world' which she built up to 'dwell in'.[11]

There is no record of Collins or of Kitty Kiernan ever having expressed the opinion that Lady Hazel was a 'fantasist'.

When Kitty was told the story of some 'society woman', she paid so little heed to it that she said she 'forgot before this' which was some weeks later, to tell him of 'something' she heard:

> Please don't misunderstand my motive. A girl friend told me that a man in Dublin told her that a girl friend of his heard from a society woman – don't know if she's a girl – in London that her only idea in life now is to get spending a night with Mick Collins. One night will do her, just for the *notoriety* of it.
>
> No wonder the thought of it makes me almost ill. Isn't England rotten? I hope Ireland won't copy England in this respect, at least get so bad. Being a simple Irish girl, I could never get used to that kind of thing, I'm sure, tho' it does seem funny, that London woman's thought of 'notoriety' at your, mine and everybody else's expense. I just thought I'd tell you what I heard. Now I'll finish sweetheart.[12]

When rumours of Michael Collins' link with Lady Hazel Lavery reached Ireland during these early days of June 1922, his opponents made full use of it. Cathal Brugha and Austin Stack found a new dimension had been added to Collins – with 'his English Lady'. They asked Todd Andrews to get in touch with Liam Tobin and have the matter investigated. 'It was well into June, when I was in a position to inform Brugha and Stack that definitely, it was only a rumour and that Collins' real sweetheart was Kitty Kiernan,' said Todd

Andrews. 'In fairness to Mick Collins he knew what he was doing, he enticed anyone – man or women – who was in a position of influence, or who would help him make inroads either into the Castle or the British Cabinet ... He would have been shot if there was any truth in the rumour that he was bedding Lady Lavery, and Brugha would not hesitate to have the order implemented.'[13]

In his autobiography, Sir John Lavery noted that Hazel had more male admirers than female when she first came to England, 'but as the years passed and no scandal could be fastened on her in any way at any time, her women admirers ... increased'.[14]

Shortly after Collins' death, on 22 August 1922, Hazel Lavery wrote to Emmet Dalton, but it was not until 15 November that Dalton responded, because her letter to him had been captured. It was retrieved when his brother Charlie Dalton, chief intelligence officer of the Treaty forces, found her letter 'amongst the many other valuable documents' on the captured Ernie O'Malley, who was an anti-Treatyite. 'It is fairly clear,' Dalton wrote to Hazel, 'that some of the Irregulars captured it in a raid on the mails in Dublin ... they retained it and evidently placed some importance upon it as they marked it "valuable document"'.[15] One method of surveillance, also used by Collins, was to rifle mail. There is no doubt that Republicans continued to view Hazel's letters as a source of internal information on government activities.

At this time – June 1922 – Hazel would continue to move in and out of Michael Collins' life but he was unaware that his former close friend Harry Boland was spying on him through Hazel. An anonymous letter to Sir John Lavery claimed: 'They have letters of hers [Hazel's] which the late Harry Boland (RIP) secured ...'[16]

In recent years Michael Collins' name has been linked romantically with another woman (in newspapers and more recent material like Mícheál Ó Cuinneagáin's, *On the Arm of Time)*. Speculation has arisen that Collins had an affair with Moya Llewelyn Davies, and it has been suggested that Collins was the father of her son Richard. I contacted her son Richard at his London office. Letters from him and a phone call confirmed that he was born (24 December 1912) before his mother met Collins. His 'knowledge' was that they were 'great friends and colleagues' and that she worked with 'Michael Collins and other Irish people to gain independence from Britain for Ireland'. In a dictated letter typed by his secretary he 'very much regrets' that 'he has no other information' which would 'help you as he would like to have been able to do so.'

Correspondence that I received from Robert Barton states: 'I regret that I am unable to give you any assistance regarding the relationship to which you refer. I should guess that it had no authenticity.' This gives the impression that he was unfamiliar with such speculation. Todd Andrews 'never heard it mentioned' and described it as 'utter nonsense'. It 'has to be pure speculation'. Andrews said that Moya was 'invaluable' to 'all of us' and did 'so much work' in the cause of 'Irish freedom'.[17]

WOMEN'S ALLEGIANCE SPLIT
BY CIVIL WAR

At a conference on 1 June 1922, Lloyd George argued that the crown was 'a mystic term' which 'simply stood for the power of the people'. Collins had another mystic term – the Republic – to contend with; he could see that failure to blot out the Crown element in the constitution had brought into sharp focus the possibility of civil war.[1]

Finally a deal was hammered out whereby the British parliament, while having reservations on the Pact, agreed that the Irish delegation should be free to pursue this course.

Collins arrived back in Ireland to an atmosphere of gloom. A meeting between Collins and de Valera in the Mansion House on 5 June resulted in a joint appeal for 'Panel candidates in the interests of national unity'. Four days later both men appeared together on a Dublin platform.

Meanwhile, fighting along the border from Belleek to Pettigo persisted between the newly established Ulster Special Constabulary and the Republican Executive Army.

On 11 June Mick asked Kitty, who was in town, to come to see him. Next morning he was in his office early 'to get a quiet minute or two ... You know I have a pretty bad week before me,' he wrote.

The constitution still needed attention. He had acquired the help of Tim Healy, Crompton Llewelyn Davies (Moya's husband), Hugh Kennedy, law officer, and James Douglas to draw up a blueprint with him, which he then submitted to the British cabinet. Mick had to go to London in a hurry on Monday evening 12 June. All next day he battled through a series of meetings in an attempt to broaden the scope of the constitution but failed to secure terms which he hoped would make it acceptable to the Republicans.

That Tuesday night, reeling in despair, he was on the boat back to Dublin. 'I did not go to bed after coming off the boat this morning,' he wrote to Kitty. Wednesday's crowded meetings with cabinet colleagues left him only a few moments to send a wire to Kitty before heading to the railway station and boarding the train for Cork. At this Cork meeting Collins severely criticised Brugha's behaviour for encouraging the army split. On the eve of election day (16 June) he again toured his Cork constituency. The constitution was published on 16 June, polling day. Throughout this month Collins was extremely busy. Dealing with constant trouble in the north-east, clashes between pro- and anti-Treaty forces, Provisional Government meetings and a huge amount of correspondence, plus having to meet so many people, consumed his summer days and nights.

The Provisional Government, with Collins as chairman, had decided that from 12 June there would be no further negotiations with their opponents, the Four Courts people, pending the formation of a new coalition, which would be further negotiated after the election.[2]

On 22 June Field-Marshal Sir Henry Wilson, military adviser to the six county administration, was assassinated outside his London home. The results of the election were announced in the aftermath of this killing on 24 June 1922: 93 pro-Treaty seats and 35 anti-Treaty Sinn Féin seats. Although Michael Collins headed the poll in his own county of Cork, he had little to be jubilant about. The new Dáil was to assemble on 1 July, and Collins could only hope for some improvement in the situation.

The month of June had been so busy that most of Mick's responses to Kitty's letters were telegrams, sent from wherever he travelled. As he had no time to visit Granard, Kitty instead came to Greystones periodically. On 24 June he sent her a telegram: 'Have finished with the counting at last. Wound up at about seven o'clock this morning. Am returning Dublin today.

Will write or wire you when I get back. How are you?'

That night, another telegram: 'Thanks for letter. I have returned safely and will write to you to-morrow'.

While he was in Granard on the Sunday the pair had a tiff, mainly due to Kitty's 'frightful misunderstandings' of Mick's inability to write her 'the long long long' letters as in the past. In London he had found the time, at the expense of sleep; more recently, sleep had become a luxury, often snatched while in transit.

Kitty realised she was her own 'worst enemy', so she promised that for his happiness as well as her own, henceforth she would try harder; 'for I do realise,' she wrote, 'how unhappy I make things for you too'.

In her letter on the day after his visit to Granard she wrote of the desire that gripped her to elope:

> I'd have stayed with you, I'd have wanted to. Last night was a real wedding night for you and me. Didn't you feel that way too, but couldn't put it into words? I wanted to run away with you. That must be the feeling with people who do run away like that. We had it last night. That was our night. Glad today for both you and me that I didn't go.[3]

Mick, again without time to write 'the long' letter which Kitty loved, said that in Greystones he had '... the first real sleep for a week. Talk of being tired – and am still very tired ...'

Affairs of state called: 'Must finish this – the usual thing! Everyone waiting, God help me – take this note for what it ought to be – about twelve pages long. God be with you, Kitty dear'.[4]

When Field-Marshal Sir Henry Wilson was shot the whole of the British Empire was shocked. Reginald Dunne and Joseph O'Sullivan of the IRA's London battalion were arrested and later charged. The Dublin cabinet, including Collins and Griffith, condemned the killing.

The British ministers incorrectly blamed the Four Courts garrison for the killing. Rory O'Connor made a public statement that he and the Four Courts men had had nothing to do with it: 'If we had, we would admit it'.

When Collins learned of the arrest of his friend Reggie Dunne and that of Joseph O'Sullivan, it created further complications for him. Although he condemned their action, he took full responsibility for their lives. In London, the event led to emergency cabinet meetings. Because the British associated the murders with the anti-Treatyites in the Four Courts, they put pressure on Collins to deal with them.

(Collins failed in his attempts to free Dunne and O'Sullivan. Their trial went ahead in the Old Bailey on 18 July. The men were found guilty and sentenced to death. In spite of Collins' appeals for a reprieve they were hanged in Wandsworth prison, London, on 10 August, 1922.)[5]

Lloyd George was no longer prepared to permit 'the ambiguous position of Rory O'Connor ... with his followers and his arsenal in open rebellion in the heart of Dublin in possession of the Courts of Justice ...' So on behalf of 'His Majesty's Government' he felt 'entitled to ask' Collins 'formally to bring it to an end forthwith'. Furthermore, his government would be prepared to place at Collins' disposal 'the necessary pieces of artillery' which might be required. Toleration of this conduct was seen as 'rebellious defiance of the principles of the Treaty ... now supported by the declared will of the Irish people'.[6]

Matters were brought to a head by news that J. J. (Ginger) O'Connell, pro-Treaty deputy chief-of-staff, had been taken hostage by Four Courts Executive forces. He was held in order to secure the release of Leo Henderson, Executive forces, who had been arrested by pro-Treaty (Provisional Government) troops as he commandeered transport at Ferguson's Garage, for removal of supplies to the north.

On Wednesday 28 June, an ultimatum was delivered to the

Four Courts garrison to surrender. That day, Mick wrote to Kitty: 'I hope the thing won't last much longer ... I do wish you'd come up for the weekend'.[7] The ultimatum brought no response so two eighteen-pounder guns borrowed from the British army opened fire on the building. The Civil War had officially begun. By Friday 30 June, the Four Courts garrison had surrendered unconditionally and many anti-Treatyites were taken prisoners.

Michael Collins' worst nightmare soon became real. His hope for the swift and speedy end to the occupation of the Four Courts and the resumption of normality dissipated. Lynch, Deasy and de Valera and a number of the Republican Executive headed south; the area south of a line stretching from Waterford to Limerick was to be held by the Republicans. Oscar Traynor took command in Dublin, where sporadic skirmishes caused much destruction.

Collins, who had done so much over the previous months to prevent a civil war, now realised he would have to be prepared to fight his friends openly. At a Provisional Government meeting on 30 June, chaired by Collins, 'It was decided that the attack on other strongholds of the Irregulars should be vigorously continued ...'[8] During the early days of July, anti-Treaty forces clashed with government forces country-wide, and it looked as though the government, the Treaty and all that Mick Collins had worked for were swiftly being eroded. Fighting had begun to spread, and like a cancer was eating into civilian life.

Throughout Dublin, Republicans had established themselves in other buildings, principally in hotels along O'Connell Street, including the Gresham. Meanwhile Maud Gonne had returned from Paris and in an effort at reconciliation had brought a group of women together. As they entered the Four Courts the garrison was due to surrender. The women then divided into two groups, one to meet Michael Collins, Griffith and Cosgrave, the other to meet the anti-Treaty side. Maud Gonne claimed that it would be on women that 'the misery of the civil war would fall'. They had a 'right to be heard', she said. But Griffith, her long-standing friend, replied, 'We are a government and we have to keep order'.[9]

The second group did not get very far with Oscar Traynor at the Hammam Hotel. It was here that Máire Comerford also came on her bicycle after she left the Four Courts. Traynor gave her some advice on changing gears; soon she had the hang of it and took off to Republican-held posts around the city to see if there were any wounded. It was at this stage that she decided definitely to throw in her lot with the anti-Treatyites.[10]

Countess Markievicz had taken up sniper duty in Moran's Hotel. Many of Collins' female friends and associates, such as Leslie Price, Linda Kearns, Grace Plunkett, Peg Barrett and her sisters, Madge Daly and her sisters, joined the opposing forces.

Cathal Brugha, with a small garrison, which included Linda Kearns, Kathleen Barry and Muriel MacSwiney, remained in the Hammam Hotel with orders to hold out until surrender was inevitable. On Tuesday, as the Hammam Hotel began to blaze under the heavy bombardment, Traynor sent a dispatch to Brugha asking him to surrender. But Brugha continued to fight like a tiger '... and fell amid a volley of shots'. Two days later he died. His friends revealed he had not intended to surrender.[11] News of Brugha's death appalled Collins. Though they were enemies latterly, he had admired the spirit and dogged determination of the older man. He understood his aggressive action, his strong-mindedness and his obstinacy.

At this time of great turmoil and stress, Mick's concern for Kitty was great, and Kitty's concern for him was heartfelt. She wrote: 'When I think of you perhaps in the midst of a fight, I think that I should be near you, beside you. Because if you were going to die, I'd like to go with you.'[12]

Caught up in the affairs of the country, he would often

only have time to send 'a very very hurried wire today' to Kitty, ' – please do forgive me for it. There are people waiting while I write it'.[13] Next day from Government Buildings: '... I'm longing to see you and everything and all my love and wherever I may be for the next week, I'll do my very best to wire and write. And God be with you, my own Kitty'.[14]

Sometimes Kitty chastised Mick for not writing more often; if she was 'really sure' that he missed her and 'had not somebody else,' she said, perhaps she would understand. Yet on reflection, it was good of him 'to write at all' and he 'so worried and upset'.[15]

With the Civil War mounting, with reports of men being killed and injured and hardships in many homes and with a million pulls on his crowded time, Mick read what he called Kitty's 'really unpleasant letter' two or three times with a heavy and sad heart. 'And who's the somebody else?' he wrote in desperation.

> And O'Connell St is broken down and I'm sorry that the poor old Gresham is gone and destroyed. But it is gone, and I suppose I can't restore it or can I or what? And what must I do? And now I'm called. So goodnight and love and everything. And if I'm in places where I can't even wire to you or where you don't hear at all of me or from me, I'll think of you and it will be all the harder because you won't know and harder still because you'll be wondering that you don't hear and all sorts of things ... And fondest love, no matter what.[16]

Matters discussed at government meetings concerned military decisions rather than political issues. In Kerry, with its long coastline and mountainous regions, anti-Treaty forces continued to train and muster military support; they took over towns and villages throughout the county and engaged in guerrilla activity. Michael Collins now decided to tackle the problem head-on; he would go back to soldiering and take command. At a government meeting on Wednesday morning 12 July, he 'announced that he had arranged to take

174

up duty as commander-in-chief of the army and would not be able to act in his ministerial capacity until further notice, and that Messrs. O'Higgins, McGrath and Fionán Lynch had also been appointed to military posts'. At this meeting W. T. Cosgrave, minister of local government, 'was appointed to act as Chairman of the Provisional Government and as Minister of Finance in the absence of Mr Collins on military duties'.[17]

During the day (12 July) he wrote to Kitty: 'I was worrying about you somehow. This is just a note, and you may not hear from me except by wire for a few days. You won't mind that – not really. I wonder when I shall see you again. May God be with you always. With all my love.' Before going to sleep that night he wrote her another note because he had got a letter from her which lacked understanding of all he had to do. The strain of work was enough: 'I've read it with a heavy and a sad heart two or three times ... Why do you think so harshly of me? It does seem strange'.[18]

Collins now had a mammoth task to restore order. He donned his military uniform and moved into quarters at Portobello Barracks.

By midnight he was 'absolutely tired and worn out after a terrible day,' he wrote in a note to Kitty. 'And I'm longing to see you and everything and all my love and, wherever I may be for the next week, I'll do my very best to wire or write. And God be with you.'[19]

Kitty saw Michael's appointment in the paper, and desperation is evident in the words she wrote: 'You are C. in Chief now. What does this mean? More trouble I suppose. Will it ever end?'[20]

He was asking himself the same question but to get the country back to stability became his principal aim. He studied army models, took advice, made plans on how a disciplined army should be structured. The organisation of payment, food supplies, clothing, arms to scattered groups of soldiers constantly on the move was a gigantic task. Tirelessly, he worked into the night hours at his Portobello desk; there are notes written at midnight and past and again at 4 or 5 in the morning. His notebook of those July days bears witness to the urgency with which he tackled most tasks and the number of items that crowded upon him. There were prison accommodation, medical service, engineering, press data, intelligence lists and a multitude of other concerns.[21]

Surrounded by war, buildings crumbling, army clashes, people being killed and injured, he wrote to Kitty, 'I have every faith in things coming right. Could not have written yesterday. Fondest love'.[22]

Collins soon discovered the sadness of civil war. Lifelong friends were becoming bitter enemies; brothers and neighbours were taking opposite sides. It wounded him when Harry Boland turned his back on him. Harry had taken a staff position in the South Dublin Brigade, but soon fled out to the Dublin hills where he wrote on 13 July to Joe McGarrity: 'It may very well be that I shall fall in this awful conflict ... I am certain we cannot be defeated even if Collins and his British Guns succeed in garrisoning every town in Ireland'.[23]

In a further note to McGarrity on 25 July Harry asked, 'Can you imagine, me on the run from Mick Collins?'[24]

On 28 July Mick wrote a heartfelt letter to Harry:

Harry – It has come to this! Of all things it has come to this.

It is in my power to arrest you and destroy you. This I cannot do. If you will think over the influence which has dominated you it should change your ideal.

You are walking under false colours. If no words of mine will change your attitude then you are beyond all hope – my hope.[25]

Mick believed that Harry had been influenced by de Valera, Brugha and Stack. On the night of 30 July, Harry dined in Jammet's Restaurant in Nassau Street with Anna Fitzsimons, who had been one of Mick's secretaries during a period prior to the Treaty. He had got Mick's letter, and was keenly aware of the changed circumstances. At one point during dinner Harry urged Anna to 'eat well,' adding, 'because it may be your last meal with me'.

That night as Harry and Joe Griffin were going to bed in the Grand Hotel in Skerries, soldiers came on a raid. Harry was injured in the stomach. He was taken to Skerries Barracks and held for four hours then moved to Portobello Barracks and on to St Vincent's Hospital.[26]

When Mick heard the news, he asked the director of intelligence to place a guard on St Vincent's Hospital, 'and to make a report on the exact condition of Mr Harry Boland' and to find out 'whether he has been operated on and what the doctors think of his condition'.[27]

Harry died on 2 August. Mick was devastated, and burst into Fionán Lynch's room in a fit of uncontrolled grief. Next day he wrote to Kitty:

> Last night I passed St Vincent's Hospital and saw a small crowd outside. My mind went in to him lying dead there and I thought of the times together, and, whatever good there is in any wish of mine, he certainly had it. Although the gap of 8 or 9 months was not forgotten – of course no one can ever forget it – I only thought of him with the friendship of the days of 1918 and 1919 ... I'd send a wreath but I suppose they'd return it torn up.[28]

Kitty, in her response to the death of 'poor Harry', wrote:

> Oh! vain is the strength of man. I realise I have lost a good friend in Harry – and no matter what, I'll always believe in his genuineness, that I was the one and only. I think you have also lost a friend. I am sure you are sorry after him. ... Always when H. was saying good-bye, he'd say 'don't worry, Kitty, Mick will be all right' ... He had my rosary beads: I have his ... Ever yours, Kitty.[29]

Mick wanted to meet Kitty for dinner, but being tied up

'in a million things' he had asked Gearóid Mac Canainn at Government Buildings to send her a wire. Harry was still on his mind. Harry's death confirmed for him the devastation of war and the inescapable price in human misery. Obviously he and Kitty had been speaking about Harry during dinner. Afterwards he wanted to clarify his position for her. He did not want any misunderstanding, so he put his thoughts on paper that night:

> ... You will not misunderstand anything you have heard me say about poor H. You'll also appreciate my feelings about the splendid men we have lost on our side, and the losses they are and the bitterness they cause, and the anguish. There is no one who feels it all more than I do.
>
> My condemnation is all for those who would put themselves up as paragons of Irish Nationality, and all the others as being not worthy of concern. May God bless you always.
> Fondest love, Mícheál.[30]

Kitty did not always sympathise with Mick's dilemmas because the burden of his work inevitably led to his neglecting her. She went to bed early one night and couldn't sleep. She thought of him and wrote:

> I was 'madly, passionately, in love with you' – to use your own words, and I understand those feelings now ... But sure you know and we both know and remember Greystones and all the other wonderful times.[31]

He tried to reassure her and to remain optimistic:

> One thing – don't worry about me. I have every faith in things coming right no matter how difficult and dark the outlook at the moment. Then we shall be happier, and I hope all the happier because of what we've been through.[32]

COMMANDER-IN-CHIEF'S AUGUST DAYS

'When are you coming to town?' Mick wrote to Kitty from government office very early on the morning of 28 July. 'You don't know [how] glad it made me to speak to you on the phone yesterday – to hear your voice and I can always feel very near one when I speak on the phone ... The pressure is very very heavy and there is little sign of relaxation.'

In his new role as commander-in-chief he was throwing himself fully into the task. In a memo to the government on the general situation on 26 July, he reported that the government forces were in a strong position. On 5 August he wrote to W. T. Cosgrave, acting chairman that he intended to deal with the immediate problems in the south. He was preoccupied with military matters, having left the political arena temporarily to Griffith, Cosgrave, O'Higgins and others.

That day he sent a telegram with his 'fondest love' to Kitty saying that it was 'quieter this morning. Hope ordinary conditions will be restored in a few days. How are you and everything? ... All here doing well so far'.

The course of the Civil War was determined by the pattern of barrack occupation of either pro- or anti-Treaty forces, and also by leaders in districts. In early August, Collins had officers and men placed in strategic positions which led to the taking of Limerick, Waterford, Wexford and other major centres. Coastal landings were suggested by Emmet Dalton, director of military operations. Dalton believed that Republican strongholds were vulnerable to attacks from the sea so Collins placed him in charge of operations to carry out his [Dalton's] own suggestion.

Michael Collins had engaged his sister, Mary Collins-Powell, to liaise between himself and Emmet Dalton in Cork. She was involved in the organisation of a volunteer force to help her brother. She was an extremely determined and efficient young women and had been a help to Mick throughout the entire revolutionary period.[1]

On this occasion Mary Collins-Powell was unable to use the direct route from Cork because of the destruction of roads and railway lines, so Harry Donegan and Dr Gerald Ahern brought her some of the way on a yacht called *The Gull*. As the wind was against them they pulled in at Waterford, which was in government hands; from there she got a taxi to Rosslare and then a train to Dublin. She had details for Michael of arrangements for the Cork landing, and told him that there were up to 500 men ready to join his forces in Cork but who were lying low due to lack of arms.[2]

On 7 August he was about to leave the barracks on army business when his sister arrived. He shared this news with Kitty: 'She [Mary Collins-Powell] is full of Cork and what the Irregulars are doing there.' They had taken control of customs duties and taxes.

Later that day, Dalton brought an eighteen-pounder and five hundred mostly raw recruits aboard the commandeered *Arvonia* and landed at Passage West, County Cork. Collins was in high spirits when he discussed the taking of west Cork with John L. O'Sullivan and Seán Hales. Both efficient soldiers, they set out by boat from Dublin with a number of men, landed without difficulty in Bantry Bay, captured the town of Bantry and took towns along the coast into Kinsale during the second week of August. These expeditions happened at the same time as a shipment force under Liam Tobin landed at Youghal, and Emmet Dalton's massive invasion of Cork city.[3]

Eoin O'Duffy, Field General of the South Western Command, moved with his men and took regions between Limerick and the North Kerry border just as General Paddy Daly landed at Fenit with 500 men on 2 August. A few days later another 240 men landed in Tarbert, so that by mid-

August the pro-Treaty troops had occupied the main centres of population in Kerry.[4]

Collins, Mulcahy and all the officials at GHQ worked for hours into the night, meeting again early in the mornings to set in motion the gigantic organisation required to get so many men transported in slow-moving boats around Irish waters.

Collins was lucky with the men with whom he worked, Richard Mulcahy, J. J. O'Connell and the officers in Dublin and countrywide were stalwarts in shouldering with him the daily burdens. There were the women of Cumann na Saoirse such as Jennie Wyse-Power, Alice Stopford-Green, Margaret O'Shea, Min Ryan, Nancy O'Brien, his sister Mary Collins-Powell and many others who did important work for him. It was after much soul-searching that many of these women supported the Treaty.

Early on 7 August Mick wrote a few of 'the most hurried lines' he had ever written to Kitty before he set out for Maryborough, the Curragh and nearby military posts. Next day he wrote to her of the harrowing experience which made him cry at the funeral Mass for nine soldiers killed in action in Kerry:

> ... the scenes at Mass were really heartbreaking. The poor women weeping and almost shrieking (some of them) for their dead sons. Sisters and one wife were there too, and a few small children. It makes one feel I tell you.[5]

With strong key men in all the commands his military tactics should soon bring the matter to a close, he was certain.

By 10 August, Dalton, with Liam Tobin and their men, was making steady progress. After hearing good news, Mick, elated, wrote a few lines to Kitty 'to show I'm thinking of you ... by this time you'll know what I had on my hands then [9 August]. Cork is in the melting pot now.'[6]

By the second week in August it was time for Collins to

move into the country to review the military posts. He was encouraged by reports returned from each of the commands that the anti-Treatyites were now 'beaten as an open force'.[7]

With this in mind, and because a sizeable part of the country was now held by the National Army, he would take a trip to the country, talk to officers and review the army on location. On Saturday, 12 August, having had little sleep, he 'left Portobello barracks at 4 am exactly' on an inspection tour. He would visit Limerick, Kerry, then cross the border into County Cork.[8]

'I am scribbling you a line and it will only be a line – as there are two officers waiting for me and a car. If, however, I don't write now I may not be back here for the post. It is very likely that you won't hear again for a few days, but you'll understand – won't you Kitty dear ... Fondest love.'[9]

His decision to travel from Kerry to Cork and other centres was halted as news reached him in Tralee late on 12 August that his friend, colleague and mentor, Arthur Griffith, had died. Very early next morning, 13 August, he was on the road again for Dublin.

Over the next few days Griffith's funeral would occupy some of Mick's time. However on Tuesday, 15 August his diary bears witness to a crowded day involving a vast number of operational matters, disciplinary matters and government correspondence.

Hazel and Sir John Lavery had come to Ireland on 13 August, and were staying at the Kingstown Hotel in Dun Laoghaire. That Wednesday morning, 16 August, Michael Collins telephoned Cosgrave before calling Sir John and Lady Hazel Lavery, both of whom had been friendly with Griffith. He met members of the Provisional Government at 10.30 am, and together they went to Arthur Griffith's funeral Mass. This was followed by the processional march to Glasnevin cemetery.[10]

That morning he had got word that Reggie Dunne and

Joseph O'Sullivan had been hanged on 10 August, in Wandsworth Prison, London, for the shooting of Sir Henry Wilson. Dunne's final wish was similar to that often expressed by Collins: 'Oh pray for our poor country!' O'Sullivan in his last letter to his mother had listed people to whom he wished to be remembered; included in the list was 'Mick Collins'.[11]

As he walked behind the tricolour-draped coffin at the head of his staff, a bystander, noticing Collins' grim expression, remarked, 'Ireland's problems hang heavily on his shoulders'.[12]

The commander-in-chief, in a graveside tribute to Arthur Griffith, said:

> He always knew what Irish Nationality meant, just as Davis knew it. He never confused it with English nationality. ... In memory of Arthur Griffith let us resolve now to give fresh play to the impulse of unity, to join together one and all in continuing his constructive work, in building up the country which he loved.[13]

This part of the task completed, he moved back. Silently he stood, head bowed, while the soil was placed over the coffin of his friend. He had more work ahead. His inspection tour of southern counties had to be completed; with most of the major towns and cities in the hands of government forces it looked to him as if the Civil War would soon be over. The slow processional march to Glasnevin had been stressful. Dr Fogarty, bishop of Killaloe, moved beside him as he stood alone and gazed at the grave. 'Michael, you should be prepared – you may be next.'

Collins turned. 'I know,' he said stoically. Then as if dismissing that interlude and wishing to God this nightmare was over, he said, 'I hope nobody takes it into his head to die for another twelve months'.[14]

Sir John and Hazel Lavery observed his despondency. They chatted with him for a few moments and asked him to join them for a meal later that night.

But first of all duty called back at his Portobello office. Later, happy to get away from his desk, he set out for the Kingstown Hotel, to have dinner with the Laverys at 8 o'clock. He was glad of the break after the ordeal of the earlier part of the day. He was never to know that Hazel had saved his life that night. Unknowingly she sat between him and the window, outside of which a gunman waited.[15]

At 10.30 pm he left for Baldonnell to pick up 'air service reports'.[16]

On Thursday morning, 17 August, he received a letter from Eoin O'Duffy, Limerick headquarters, stating that Mr Liam Hayes TD had brought O'Duffy a letter requesting that Commandant General Hannigan issue to Dan Breen, 'a safe conduct' pass to see Collins. O'Duffy argued: 'I respectfully suggest that you refuse to see him. He has been most active against us here and was one of the great "ralliers" in the fight put up by the Irregulars' and is 'the tool of Lynch' who in turn is 'the tool' of de Valera. 'Any sort of negotiations at this stage would do an enormous amount of damage among the troops. They would immediately ease off and it would take some time to get them back to the present fighting spirit.'

In this letter O'Duffy explained how much territory was now held by the National Force. With himself moving along the front from 'the Waterford border to Rathmore' in Kerry, with Dalton taking in much of the Cork area and Prout moving from Waterford towards Clonmel and on, 'with all three ... working in co-operation for a week, which should bring us up to the 25th August, we might then be in a position to negotiate with advantage ... I suggest to you, not to see Breen or any of the others ...'[17]

This opinion from a commanding officer like O'Duffy, together with the aerial reconnaissance report and a further report from Dalton of the capture of the Mallow-Fermoy-Buttevant area, helped Collins to clarify his thoughts.

He felt he should resume his review of the forces in the

south, see the situation for himself, and speak to officers 'on the ground'. Immediately he sent a message to O'Duffy: 'Am anxious to know progress towards Millstreet. Expect to see you linked up with Dalton everywhere within twenty-four hours. See you about ten o'clock on Saturday.' His mind was made up. At this juncture he wasn't sure how far south he would go, but he was going south – first to Limerick.[18]

Early next morning, Friday 18 August, he walked into the office of Joe McGrath, his intelligence officer, and announced his intention of travelling south. McGrath protested, pointing out the danger.

On one occasion Mick had said to Cosgrave, 'Do you think I shall live through this [Civil War]? Not likely!' And he turned to Sinéad Mason and asked, 'How would you like a new boss?' She found this so strange that she recounted the episode to O'Reilly. Next day as the two were out, O'Reilly enquired about his health, 'Rotten,' replied Collins. There was a slight pause, 'How would you like a new boss?' O'Reilly's heart sank. He told him he would never work for anybody else. Never a man to dwell on anything, Collins had an order for O'Reilly then, and the incident was forgotten.[19]

Now this morning Collins had another order. He told McGrath to get a convoy organised; he was determined he was not 'going to run from his own Corkmen'. He would travel on Sunday, not on Saturday as he initially intended, as an amount of correspondence awaited his attention.

McGrath later wrote all his objections in red ink in a letter which he intended to put on Collins' desk, but on reflection decided that when Collins gave an order he wanted it implemented without argument.

Next morning a wire message from Dalton in Cork stated that 'terms' had been communicated to him 'by a committee of prominent citizens of Cork'. Their terms included a week's truce during which 'facilities are to be afforded to the Republican military and political leaders to hold a meeting to discuss the making of peace.' Certain guidelines concerning 'arms, ammunitions and political prisoners' were listed in a five-point plan.[20]

Collins responded by wire:

> Will you say by cypher who the prominent citizens responsible for the offer are? Have the Irregular Leaders, political and military agreed to the offer and is it made on their behalf?
>
> Government offer published in the Press 5 June and conveyed to the People's Rights Association, Cork stands.

So that there would be no ambiguity, Collins listed the terms which included the 'Transfer into the national armoury of all war materials'.[21]

Collins as commander-in-chief knew now that he was acting from a position of strength: 'Any further blood is on their [the Anti-Treatyites] shoulders. The onus is placed unmistakably on their shoulders,' he wrote.[22]

That Saturday morning Lady Hazel Lavery telephoned Elizabeth, Countess of Fingall and asked if she thought Sir Horace Plunkett would like her 'to bring Michael Collins over to supper'. A number of important people had been invited to dinner at Kilteragh House, residence of Sir Horace Plunkett, who was the founder of the cooperative movement.

The countess replied that she was sure Sir Horace as well as George Bernard Shaw who had also been invited would be 'interested in the idea of meeting the rebel leader'.[23]

In Portobello Barracks that same morning Michael Collins was feeling unwell. As he sat down to breakfast beside Richard Mulcahy he was 'writhing with pain from a cold all through his body; and yet he was facing his day's work for that Saturday, and facing his Sunday's journey.'[24]

While he attended to some preliminaries in his office he got a telephone call from Lady Hazel Lavery inviting him to the Plunkett dinner. He gladly accepted. Shortly afterwards he left the barracks. He had a few calls to make and dropped in briefly on his friends, the Leigh Doyles, in Greystones, where with Kevin O'Higgins and others he had been a regular visitor. Kitty often stayed there when visiting Dublin. She would come again at the weekend, and he would meet her on his return from his army tour of inspection. He asked them 'to take care of her' – afterwards this would have ominous significance, as neither would ever see him again. On the way he had picked up a picture of himself in uniform which had been taken recently on Portobello grounds. He gave them a copy; he would sign it when he returned from Cork. Now he was in a hurry. Kitty had written that she had got a wire to go to her sister Chrys in Belfast who had had a baby though it wasn't due until 'end of August or later ... Picture my disappointment,' she wrote. 'I intended going to town this week ... I've got a feeling that I'll be lonely this time and not interested'.[25]

Back in his office he dealt with a vast amount of correspondence. There were also last-minute decisions to be made regarding his next day's journey. Although he was not in top form physically he got through a tremendous volume of work, including a large number of letters.

Later in the evening, having checked with Joe McGrath that everything was in order for his early morning start, he was ready to relax for a few hours. According to Sir John Lavery, Hazel was anxious that Horace Plunkett and Michael Collins should meet. She took Collins 'the same evening alone. I was a little anxious,' Sir John wrote, 'but for some reason did not go'.[26] Lennox Robinson, who was also there, afterwards wrote to Lady Gregory: 'He came in Lady Lavery's train, or rather she in his, for she is his abject admirer'.[27]

That night prior to his southern tour, Collins signed his name in the visitor's book at Kilteragh House, in the now familiar manner, Mícheál Ó Coileáin – the Irish version. Because he was quieter than usual he did not impress Countess Elizabeth – 'not at all an eloquent man, and my recollection of the dinner is that it was very quiet, and almost dull.'[28]

The writer, George Bernard Shaw, met him that night 'for the first and last time'. He was 'very glad' he did. 'I rejoice in the memory,' he wrote afterwards to Lady Lavery.[29]

The guests, who included W. T. Cosgrave, left early because Michael Collins had to leave early for his journey south. They went 'for a drive in the mountains,' according to Sir John Lavery – 'a car with an escort followed them'. As they returned to the Kingstown Hotel where the Laverys were staying, they were ambushed. 'Half a dozen shots were poured into the car.'[30]

On their arrival at the hotel Sir John examined the car with an electric torch: 'It seemed a miracle that no one was hurt, for there were six people in the car, sitting close together.' Collins' slight illness caused him to make light of the ambush; he was complaining of a pain in his side and thought it might be 'his appendix'. After some persuasion he accepted Sir John's offer of a hot-water bottle which he placed under his tunic. He smiled and said, 'The pain is gone'. With a 'God bless you both,' he jumped into the car which sped off into the night. That was the last time that Lady Hazel and Sir John saw Michael Collins alive.[31]

When he reached Portobello Barracks, Mick told Joe O'Reilly how badly he had been feeling. O'Reilly made a hot drink with oranges and took it to his colleague in bed.

'God that's grand!' said Collins with glee.

These words of gratitude encouraged O'Reilly, who on impulse bent down to tuck him in for the night. Not used to such personal touches, Collins gathered his strength and shouted, 'Go to hell and leave me alone!'[32]

'If only this thing was over I'd feel quite happy but I'm afraid I might lose you before I've really had you,' Kitty had written at the beginning of August as she recalled the first anniversary of their going-out together.

Mick had cherished the peace of the Truce period, following the hair-raising days of the War of Independence, when he could spend week-ends in Granard, attend Horse Show week and spend some days with Kitty. Now he longed for those days again, despite their having been laced with the anxiety of winning her love. More and more he had to depend now on Kitty's letters and on her coming to Dublin – 'but you will write, won't you? When are you coming up again? You said next week. And it's next week now. It is you know. And when are you coming?' he pleaded on 8 August. He had to be himself, in control; if his tasks scooped from his rest-time it wasn't important because ever since childhood he would endeavour to give his best.

> Kitty – you won't be cross with me for the way I go around. I can't help it and if I were to do anything else it wouldn't be me, and I really couldn't stand it. And somehow I feel the way I go on is better. And please, please do not worry.[33]

Kitty agreed she'd 'try not to worry tho' it's hard not to,' as she was 'as fond' of him 'as ever', she said. She had gone to see him that weekend and she 'never felt before' that she was 'such pals' with him. His communication with Kitty was now all done in the haste of his tumbling schedule. When he complained that she didn't write often enough, she put the blame on the post, 'I wrote on Tuesday and since, but it takes two days to get to Dublin, damn it. I am sorry as I'd love you to get my letters in time. I was delighted with even your *little* note, and am longing to see you. Years and years since Saturday!' she wrote on 15 August.[34]

Kitty intended travelling to Dublin after she had visited her sister Chrys in Bangor. She longed for one of 'those long chats' when they would plan their future, a future with children, with hope, with love. Because of the troubled times the date of their planned June wedding had come and gone. But the day would not be far off, Mick felt.[35]

His cold was only incidental, his duty as commander-in-chief of the army of the Provisional Government was now his priority. Having drunk O'Reilly's hot orange, he would have a good, though short, night's sleep and be ready to tackle the demanding journey and review of troops in many barracks.

Michael Collins woke early on Sunday 20 August, 1922. He dressed hastily. He and his convoy went through Limerick on to Mallow, to Cork. He stayed in the Imperial Hotel, where he met his friend Emmet Dalton and his sister Mary Collins-Powell. The following day, Monday 21 August, he was engaged in government business in Cork, then travelled to Cobh and later Macroom on army inspections. That night he again stayed at the Imperial Hotel. The next morning, 22 August, he and his party left the hotel at 6.15 am for his inspection tour of army barracks in west Cork. He visited his home area, Sam's Cross, and met his favourite aunt, his brother, cousins, friends and family members. On his way back to Cork City, travelling by the only route open to him, he was ambushed and shot dead at Béal na mBláth.

(A detailed account of the last three days of Michael Collins' life and an analysis of the way in which he met his death and of subsequent events are contained in my The Day Michael Collins Was Shot)

DEEP MOURNING FOR LOVER
AND LEADER

On Wednesday morning 23 August, Elizabeth Countess of Fingall was sitting with Bernard Shaw's wife beside the fire in the study at Kilteragh House where Michael Collins had dined with them just a few nights previously. Suddenly the door opened and Hazel appeared 'in deep mourning'.

'I knew it before I saw the papers,' she said, 'I had seen him in a dream, his face covered with blood.'

On Thursday morning, Lady Hazel and Countess Elizabeth went to view the body at the chapel of the Sisters of Charity at St Vincent's Hospital. Tall candles burned at his head and feet while four soldiers 'guarded him in his last sleep. Michael Collins lay in full uniform, and to him death had given her full measure of beauty and dignity, increased by the effect of that white bandage round his head, which hid the wound made by the bullet that had killed him. His face had taken on an almost Napoleonic cast,' said Countess Elizabeth. When she whispered to one of the soldiers, 'Where had he been hit?' he responded by touching the back of his own head.

The two young women with tear-stained faces stood for some time in silent prayer and then left.[1]

A short while later, Kitty Kiernan entered the little chapel, accompanied by her sister. Kitty's eyes were red with crying. Now tears poured down her cheeks. She kissed Mick, held him and looked down at him for a long, long time.

Mick's friend Oliver Gogarty had embalmed the body and Albert Power made a death-mask of him. Sir John Lavery now began to do a painting of him. Later the remains were ceremoniously taken in procession to City Hall for the public lying-in-state. Queues filed past – members of the Squad, his intelligence men, government ministers, army officers and his many close comrades who had worked and suffered with him since 1915. On Sunday evening 27 August the body was taken to the pro-cathedral and the following morning, after Requiem Mass, the funeral cortège set out on the six-mile journey to Glasnevin cemetery. The coffin bore a single white lily, last symbol of Kitty's love. Thousands lined the streets to pay their last respects.

On that August morning in Glasnevin Mick Collins' sisters, Hannie, Margaret, Mary and Katie, his brother Johnny and many of Collins' comrades in arms and in politics now stood at the graveside – men like Dalton, Mulcahy, Dolan, O'Reilly, Cosgrave, O'Higgins, Blythe, Tobin, Cullen, O'Duffy, women like Jennie Wyse-Power, Min Ryan, Moya Llewelyn Davies.

Richard Mulcahy, who would afterwards take Michael Collins' place as commander-in-chief of the army, was almost poetic when he delivered the oration over his dead friend, now laid to rest beside other Volunteer friends:

> Tom Ashe, Thomas MacCurtain, Traolach MacSuibhne, Dick McKee, Mícheál Ó Coileáin, and all of you who lie buried here, disciples of our great Chief, those of us you leave behind are all, too, grain from the same handful ... Men and women of Ireland, we are all mariners on the deep, bound for a port still seen only through storm and spray, sailing still on a sea 'full of dangers and hardships, and bitter toil'. But the Great Sleeper lies smiling in the stern of the boat, and we shall be filled with that spirit which will walk bravely upon the waters.[2]

This oration was recorded by Patrick O'Driscoll (husband of Collins' sister Margaret and a reporter in Dáil Éireann) on the blank page at the back of his prayer book.

In one of the last letters that Kitty wrote to Mick, she expressed her sorrow on the death of Arthur Griffith and wondered if he [Griffith] had been 'prepared'.

'I am always thinking of you and worrying,' she wrote, that 'you'll be shot, but God is very good to you.'

Just over a week later she was standing at his graveside.

The candles Mick had lit for Kitty in the churches of London and Dublin and the candles she had lit for him were now a memory. But Kitty would continue throughout her life to light a candle for him.

Two tearful women met for the first time. Michael Collins' fiancée Kitty Kiernan and his dear friend Lady Hazel Lavery spontaneously embraced. Other friends and relatives sobbed softly.[3]

To the remaining members of the Provisional Government and officers in the army was left the task of picking up the threads of Michael Collins' work.

POSTSCRIPT

Shortly after the funeral George Bernard Shaw wrote to Hannie, Michael Collins' sister:

> Don't let them make you miserable about it: how could a born soldier die better than at the victorious end of a good fight, falling to the shot of another Irishman – a damned fool, but all the same an Irishman who thought he was fighting for Ireland – 'a Roman to a Roman'? ...
>
> So tear up your mourning and hang up your brightest colours in his honour; and let us all praise God that he had not to die in a snuffy bed of a trumpery cough, weakened by age, and saddened by the disappointments that would have attended his work had he lived.[1]

Lady Hazel Lavery and her husband returned to England in September 1922. She invited Kevin O'Higgins to her entertainments whenever business took him to London.[2] W. T. Cosgrave commissioned Sir John to paint a portrait of her, which graced the Irish pound note for many years. Cosgrave said, 'Every Irishman, not to mention the foreigner who visits Ireland, will carry [Lady Hazel] next to his heart.'

Her husband Sir John wrote: 'Her rare beauty of face and character must have been known personally to be believed. We had twenty-five years together. She died in 1935, after a long illness'.[3]

Kitty Kiernan was the woman most grievously affected by Mick's death. *The Evening Mail* of 23 August and *The Irish Independent* of 24 August commented on Michael Collins' planned marriage to Kitty:

> In the midst of the national grief occasioned by his death a due share of sympathy will go out to this young lady in the irreparable loss she has sustained ... They became attached under romantic circumstances. One occasion she tramped all through the night to a lonely cabin where General Collins was

hiding, and warned him that the Auxiliaries were on their way to arrest him.

Not long after his death Kitty recovered the letters she had written to Mick over a twelve-month period. Throughout her life she kept those letters as well as his letters near her so that she could read them over and over. Because she moved house on a few occasions some of the letters got mislaid, and she destroyed others for personal reasons about which we can only speculate.

In 1925 Kitty met and married Felix Cronin. He was also a veteran of the War of Independence and the Civil War, and as with other men of the time, he had met Mick Collins and fallen under the spell of 'the big fellow'. Kitty and Felix had two sons.

As well as her treasured letters, she had the portrait of Michael Collins that had been painted by Sir John Lavery in London during the Treaty negotiations. This she set on an easel in her main living-room wherever she lived.

Though the portrait did not apparently give rise to any difficulty between the pair, their life together was not altogether happy. At times Felix drank to excess and Kitty was often moody; she tended to create the 'misunderstandings and little rows' so well known to Mick Collins. She suffered from hypertension and other ailments, particularly in her latter years. She died on 24 July 1945, and is buried in Glasnevin Cemetery, not far from where Michael Collins was laid to rest. Sixteen years later Felix joined her.

Her collection of letters, including her love letters, were offered for public auction by her two sons, Michael Collins Cronin and Felix Cronin, on 13 June 1995. They were purchased by Peter Barry.

NOTES

From Woodfield to London
1 Helena Collins, *Memoir*, 4 /9/1970.
2 Helena Collins, 4/9/1970. (Ellen Collins, a cousin, was head teacher of the girls' school).
3 Michael O'Brien to author, 15/12/73.
4 Helena Collins, *op. cit.*, 4/9/1970.
5 Michael Collins to Kevin O'Brien, 16/10/1916, q. Rex Taylor, *Michael Collins*, pp. 25, 26.

Friendships and Organisations
1 Piaras Béaslaí, *Michael Collins*, V. 1, p. 13.
2 P. S. O'Hegarty, The *Victory of Sinn Féin*, p. 24.
3. Elizabeth Countess of Finall, *Seventy Years Young*, pp. 50, 55. Telephone conversation (26 Sept. 1974) with Richard Llewelyn Davies (born 1912) confirm that Collins met Moya Llewelyn Davies first in late 1913.
4. *Ibid.*, pp. 50–55, 409.
5. *Ibid.*, pp. 50–55. 402, 403.
6 Michael Collins to Hayden Talbot, q. *Michael Collins' Own Story*, p. 26.
7 *Ibid.*
8 Ned Barrett to author, June 1974 (details of Knocknacurra visit); Michael Collins, *The Proof of Success*, p. 54.

Easter 1916
1 Michael to Susan Killeen, 19/10/1915, private letters, Máire Molloy.
2 Michael to Hannie, 17/1/1916 and 27/1/1916.
3 *Ibid.*, 29/1/1916.
4. 1916 Proclamation.
5 Michael to Hannie, 16/5/1916.
6 *Ibid.*
7 Michael to Susan Killeen, 27/5/1916.
8 *Ibid.*
9 Ned Barrett (Kilbrittain), June 1974.

10 Michael to Nancy O'Brien, 26/7/1916, Liam O'Donoghue, also J. O'Brien private papers.
11 Michael to Hannie, 25/8/1916.
12 Piaras Béaslaí, *op. cit.*, p. 116.
13 Collins to Seán Deasy, 12/10/1916.
14 Michael to Susan Killeen, 21/9/1916.
15 Ned Barrett to author, 1/6/1974.
16 Michael O'Brien to author, 8/12/1973.
17 Michael to Susan Killeen, 31/12/1916.
18 Mary Collins-Powell, *Memoir*.

Women Aid IRB Reorganisation
1 Michael to Hannie, 23/1/1917.
2 Michael Collins, *How Ireland Made Her Case Clear*, p. 60.
3 Kathleen Clarke, *Revolutionary Woman*, p. 142.
4 *Ibid.*
5 Michael to Hannie, 8/10/1917.
6 *Ibid.*

The Pulse of the Secret Service
1 Michael Collins' prison journal, April 1919, held by Íosold Ó Deirg, daughter of Sinéad Mason, Collins' secretary.
2 *Ibid.*, April 1919.
3 Michael to Hannie, 10/4/1918.
4 Kathleen Clarke, *op. cit.*, p. 150.
5 Michael to Hannie, 20/4/1918.
6 Ministry of Defence Archives, Ireland.
7 Diana Norman, *Terrible Beauty: a Life of Constance Markievicz*, p. 188.
8 Frank O'Connor, *The Big Fellow*, p. 56.
9 Michael to his sister Helena 13/4/1919, John Pierce private papers.
10 *Ibid.*

Intelligence-gathering Continues
1 Dave Neligan to author, 10/1/1974.
2 Michael Collins (Nancy O'Brien's son) to author, 5/3/1986.
3 Nancy O'Brien-Collins, 'Recollections' in *Irish Independent* Supplement, 20/8/1966.
4 Piaras Béaslaí, *Irish Independent*, 20/8/1966.

5   Florrie O'Donoghue, *Irish Independent*, 20/8/1966; I am
    indebted in John Borgonovo for details regarding reuniting
    Josephine Marchmount and her son Reggie. Other quotes
    are from interviews with Criostóir de Baróid 12/1/1981 and
    Margaret Helen 18/7/1984.
6   Piaras Béaslaí, *Irish Independent*, 20/8/1966.

Women Linchpin in Espionage
1   Robert Barton to Moya Llewelyn Davies, 13/6/1919.
2   Máire Comerford to author, 5/9/1979.
3   Foregoing story by Piaras Béaslaí, *Irish Independent*, 20/8/
    1966.
4   *The Police Gazette, Hue-And-Cry*, 28/12/1920.
5   Alice Stopford Green, *Ireland's Pride and Ireland's Sorrow*, p.
    45.
6   Margery Forester, *The Lost Leader*, p. 121.
7   Michael Collins' prison journal, April 1919.
8   Dave Neligan to author, 29/1/1974.
9   Harry Boland to Michael Collins, q. S. Ó Muirthile, *Memoirs*,
    p. 78.
10 Dave Neligan to author, 29/1/1974.
11 Mícheál Ó Coileáin to Dónal Hales, 25/2/1920, Hales private
    papers.
12 Collins to Hayden Talbot, q. Talbot, *op. cit.*, p. 78.
13 Harry Boland to Kitty Kiernan, 17/6/1920.
14 Todd Andrews to author, 4/11/1983.
15 Dorothy (Dicker) Heffernan, records and reminiscences.

The Heart of British Intelligence
1   Collins to Dónal Hales, 13/8/1920.
2   *Ibid.*
3   Máire Comerford to author, 4/9/1979.
4   *Ibid.*
5   Kathleen Napoli MacKenna, *Memoir*, q. Tim Pat Coogan,
    Michael Collins, p. 108.
6   Piaras Béaslaí, *op. cit.*, V. 1, p. 427.
7   Dan Breen, *My Fight for Irish Freedom*, p. 152.
8   Frank O'Connor, *op. cit.*, p. 119.
9   Dorothy Macardle, *The Irish Republic*, p. 368.
10 Michael Collins to Hayden Talbot, Talbot, *op. cit.*, p. 93.

11 Richard Mulcahy, Notes on Béaslaí's *Michael Collins*, MP, UCDA.

12 Dorothy (Dicker) Heffernan to author, 10/9/1996.

13 Collins to McKee, q. Rex Taylor, *op. cit.*, pp. 98,104.

14 T. Ryle Dwyer, *Michael Collins: the Man Who Won the War*, p. 100.

15 Rex Taylor, *op. cit.*, p. 100.

16 Original in Kilmainham Museum.

17 Leslie Price, 3/7/1979, and Máire Comerford, 4/9/1979, to author.

18 Collins to Boland, q. Rex Taylor, *op cit.*, p. 96.

19 Michael Collins to *Irish Independent*, 7/12/1920.

20 *Ibid.*

21 Piaras Béaslaí, *op. cit.*, pp. V. 11, 139, 140, also Batt O'Connor, *With Michael Collins in the Fight for Irish Freedom*, pp. 120, 121.

Women's Gun-running Role

1 Collins to Griffith, 26/1/1921.

2 Peg Barrett to author, April 1976.

3 Michael to his sister, Helena (Sr Mary Celestine) 5/3/1921.

4 Frank O'Connor, *op. cit.*, p. 117.

5 Dorothy (Dicker) Heffernan to author, 10/9/1996.

6 Madge Hales to author, 20/6/1972.

7 Richard Mulcahy, 'Note on the Differences', *Studies* LXVII No. 267 (Autumn 1978), p. 190.

8 Leslie Price de Barra, private papers, also Leslie Price to author, June 1979. During the Truce, Leslie married Tom Barry.

9 Liam O'Donoghue to author, September 1980.

10 Michael to Helena, 5/3/1921.

11 Dave Neligan to author 11/2/1974.

Raids, Arrests, Suspicion of Betrayal

1 Michael to Helena, 5/3/1921.

2 Michael to Mary Collins-Powell, 24/3/1921.

3 Collins to Art O'Brien, 21/3/1921 and 4/5/1921.

4 Kathleen Napoli MacKenna, National Library of Ireland.

5 Details of Brigid Lyons and Seán MacEoin from interview with

Máire Comerford, 4/9/1979; see also Coogan, *Michael Collins*, pp. 180, 181. Collins to the Brigade Adjutant, Cork No. 3 Brigade, 7/4/1921, Meda Ryan, *The Tom Barry Story*, p. 73.

6   Michael to Helena, 5/3/21.
7   Michael O'Brien to author, 15/12/1973.
8   Collins to *Freeman's Journal*, 22/4/1921.
9   Batt O'Connor, *op. cit.*, p. 76.
10 Collins to de Valera, 1/6/1921.
11 Collins to Moya Llewelyn Davies, 9/6/1921.
12 *Ibid.*, 24/6/1921.
13 Collins to Dónal Hales, 7/7/1921.
14 Madge Hales to author, 20/6/1972.
15 Thornton *Memoir*.
16 T. Ryle Dwyer, *De Valera, The Man and the Myth*, p. 55.
17 *Ibid.*, p. 55, 60.

Truce, Intrigue, Treaty Negotiations

1   Collins to Moya Llewelyn Davies, 23/7/1921.
2   *Ibid.*
3   Collins to de Valera, 19/7/1921.
4   Collins to Moya Llewelyn Davies, 9/7/1921.
5   Michael to Kitty, 2/8/1921, Kitty Kiernan letters, Peter Barry private collection.
6   *Ibid.*, 21/8/1921.
7   *Ibid.*, 22/8/1921.
8   *Ibid.*, 31/8/1921.
9   Collins to Moya Llewelyn Davies, 31/8/1921.
10 *Ibid.*
11 Harry Boland to Kitty Kiernan, 8/9/1921, Kitty Kiernan letters, Peter Barry private collection.
12 *Morning Post*, 5/9/1921.
13 Michael to Kitty, 6/9/1921.
14 Harry Boland to Kitty, 8/9/1921.
15 *Ibid.*, 20/9/1921.
16 *Ibid.*
17 Piaras Béaslaí, *op. cit.*, p. 275, also T. Ryle Dwyer, *Michael Collins and the Treaty*, p. 46.
18 Piaras Béaslaí, *op. cit.*, p. 275.
19 Michael to Kitty, 29/9/1921.
20 Frank Pakenham, *Peace by Ordeal*, pp. 87, 88.

21 *Ibid.*
22 de Valera to McGarrity, 27/12/1921, J. McGarrity papers, MS 17,440, NLI.
23 Florence O'Donoghue, *No Other Law*, p. 192; Meda Ryan, *Liam Lynch: the Real Chief*, p. 88.

Love Triangle
1 Harry Boland to Kitty, 1/10/1921.
2 *Ibid.*
3 *Ibid.*, 2/10/1921.
4 K. Boland to Kitty, 4/10/1921.
5 Michael to Kitty, 5/10/1921.
6 *Ibid.*, 8/10/1921.
7 *Ibid.*, 9/10/1921.
8 *Ibid.*, 9/10/1921.
9 *Daily Express*, 12/10/1921.
10 Michael to Kitty, 11/10/1921.
11 *Ibid.*, 12/10/1921.
12 Harry Boland to Kitty, 11/10/1921.
13 Michael to Kitty, 12/10/1921.
14 *Ibid.*, 13/10/1921.
15 Harry Boland to Kitty, 14/10/1921.
16 Michael to Kitty, 14/10/1921.
17 *Ibid.*, 14/10/1921 and 15/10/1921.
18 Harry Boland to Kitty, n. d.
19 Michael to Kitty, 16/10/1921.
20 Harry Boland to Kitty 11/10/1921.
21 Michael to Kitty, 16/10/1921.
22 *Ibid.*, 17/10/1921.
23 Harry Boland to Kitty, 14/10/1921.
24 Kitty to Michael, n. d.
25 Michael to Kitty, 17/10/1921.
26 *Ibid.*, 19/10/1921.
27 *Ibid.*, 20/10/1921.
28 *Ibid.*, 20/10/1921.
29 *Ibid.*, 20/10/1921.
30 Kitty to Michael, 14/10/1921.
31 *Ibid.*
32 Kitty to Michael, n. d., written in pencil for which she apologises.

33 Michael to Kitty, 16/10/1921.

34 Kitty to Michael, n. d.

35 *Ibid.*

36 Michael to Kitty, n. d.

37 Kitty to Michael, n. d.

38 Michael to Kitty, 23/10/1921.

39 *Ibid.*, 24/10/1921.

40 Kathleen Napoli MacKenna, *Memoirs*, NLI.

41 Michael to Kitty, Cadogan Gardens, 12.30 am. n.d.

London Society and Conferences

1 Michael to Kitty, n. d. c. end October 1921.

2 Collins to John O'Kane, 23/10/1921.

3 Collins to John O'Kane, 17/10/1921.

4 Mark Sturgis' *Diary*.

5 Michael to Kitty, 8/1/1921.

6 Ernie O'Malley, *The Singing Flame*, p. 34.

7 Leon Ó Broin, p. 96.

8 Michael to Kitty, 9/11/1921.

9 James Douglas to Collins, Collins Papers, NLI.

10 Michael to Kitty, 15/11/1921.

11 Collins to O'Kane, 14/11/1921.

12 Michael to Kitty, 15/11/1921.

13 *Ibid.*, 16/11/1921.

14 Sir John Lavery, *The Life of a Painter*, pp. 189, 190, 208.

15 *Ibid.*, pp. 205–207.

16 *Ibid.*, p. 213.

17 Michael to Kitty, 16/11/1921.

18 Sir John Lavery, *op cit.*, pp. 213, 214, 215.

19 Countess of Fingall, *op. cit.*, p. 402.

20 Sir John Lavery, *op. cit.*, p. 214.

21 Oliver St John Gogarty, *As I Was Going Down Sackville Street*,
   p. 241.

22 Emmet Dalton to author, 20/4/1974.

23 Countess of Fingall, *op. cit.*, p. 403.

24 Collins to O'Kane, 15/11/1921.

25 Margery Forester, *op. cit.*, *p.* 242.

26 Rex Taylor, *op cit.*, *p.* 135.

Letters – In Great Haste

1   Richard Mulcahy, *Studies* LXVII No. 267 (Autumn 1978), p. 190.
2   Michael to Kitty (Wicklow Hotel), 25/11/1921.
3   Michael to Kitty, 28/11/1921.
4   *Ibid.*, 30/11/1921.
5   Collins to O'Kane, 29/11/1921.
6   Michael to Kitty, 1/12/1921.
7   Kitty to Michael, 30/11/1921.
8   *Ibid.*, 1/12/1921.
9   Childers' Diary, Trinity College Dublin Archives.
10 Dáil, Private Sessions, p. 104.
11 Frank O'Connor, *op. cit.*, p. 168.
12 Michael to Kitty, 4/12/1921.
13 Tom Jones, *Whitehall Diary*, pp. 178–180.
14 Sir John Lavery, *op. cit.*, p. 214.
15 Collins to O'Kane, 30/11/21.
16 For a fuller account of the Treaty Negotiations, see Thomas Pakenham, *Peace by Ordeal*, also T. Ryle Dwyer, *Michael Collins and the Treaty*.
17 Collins to O'Kane, n. d.
18 Robert Barton, Report on sub-conference, 5/12/1921 and 6/12/1921.
19 Scott, *Political Diaries*, p. 412.
20 Thomas Pakenham, *op. cit.*, p. 237.
21 Sir Austen Chamberlain, *Down the Years*, p. 236.
22 *Ibid.*
23 Childers' Diary, TCD.
24 Kathleen Napoli MacKenna to Leon Ó Broin, q. Ó Broin, *Michael Collins*, p. 111.
25 Frederick Birkenhead, *The Life of F. E. Smith*, p. 163.

Lady Lavery Spies on British Cabinet

1   Barbara Cartland, *We Danced All Night*, p. 127.
2   Michael to Kitty, 5/12/1921 and 6/12/1921.
3   Batt O'Connor, *op. cit.*, pp. 180 – 182.
4   Piaras Béaslaí, *op. cit.*, pp. V. II, 311.
5   Longford and O'Neill, *Éamon de Valera*, p. 168.
6   Emmet Dalton to author, 20/4/1974.
7   Lady Hazel Lavery to Michael Collins, c. 10/12/1921, Kitty

Kiernan letters, Peter Barry private collection.

8 *Ibid.*

9 Collins to O'Kane, 4/11/1922; see earlier context.

10 Lady Hazel Lavery to Michael Collins, c. 10/12/1921.

11 *Ibid.*, c. 14/12/1921.

12 *Ibid.*

13 Sinéad McCoole, *Hazel, A Life of Lady Lavery*, p. 87.

14 Emmet Dalton to author, 20/4/1974. Letter of 14/1/1921 sent
   via Sir Ed. Marsh.

15 Tim Pat Coogan, *op. cit.*, p. 289.

16 Kilmainham Museum, Ms 964A.

17 Emmet Dalton to author, 20/4/1974. It was with reluctance
   that Dalton parted with this information.

18 Ulick O'Connor, *Sunday Independent*, 15/9/1996.

19 Hazel Lavery to Michael Collins, 14/12/1921; undated fragment sent to Hazel from Hannie, Kilmainham Museum.

20 Sir John Lavery, *op. cit.*, p. 262; Tom Jones, *Whitehall Diary*,
   pp. 118, 150.

21 Kitty to Michael, 14/12/1921.

22 Michael to Kitty, 15/12/1921.

Turmoil in the Dáil

1 Michael to Kitty, 16/12/1921.

2 *Ibid.*, 17/12/1921.

3 *Ibid.*, 18/12/1921.

4 Kitty to Michael, 15/12/1921.

5 *Ibid.*, 17/12/1921.

6 Michael to Kitty, 20/12/1921.

7 Margery Forester, *op. cit.*, pp. 271.

8 *Ibid.*, p. 273.

9 Michael to Kitty, 3/1/1922.

Treaty Divides Friends

1 Michael to Kitty, 3/1/1922.

2 *Ibid.*, 6/1/1922.

3 *Ibid.*, 9/1/1922.

4 *Ibid.*, 10/1/1922.

5 *Ibid.*, 11/1/1922.

6 *Ibid.*, 16/1/1922.

7 *Ibid.*, 6/1/1922.

8   Harry Boland to Kitty, 10/1/1922.
9   *Irish Independent*, 6/2/1922.
10 Brother Allen Papers, O'Connell Schools.
11 Michael to Kitty, 21/1/1922.
12 Collins to O'Kane, 21/1/1922.
13 Juliet Duff to Leonie Leslie q. Sinéad McCoole, *op. cit.*, p. 85. (Date in footnote is given as 23 January although Collins was back in Dublin on 23 January)
14 Collins Papers, NLI.
15 Michael to Kitty, 29/1/1922.
16 *Ibid.*, 27/1/1922.

Love, Turmoil, Crowded Schedule
1   Michael to Kitty (London), 4/2/1922.
2   *Ibid.*, 5/2/1922.
3   Cutting from The *Liverpool Express*, sent with letter to Kitty by Fr Malachy, a cousin in Liverpool, 9/2/1922.
4   Michael to Kitty from London, 15/2/1922 (He enquires if she has been reading this book).
5   Michael to Kitty, 27/2/1922.
6   Kitty to Michael, 28/2/1922.
7   Michael to Kitty, 29/2/1992.
8   Kitty to Michael, 28/2/1922.
9   *Ibid.*, 14/2/1922.
10 Michael to Kitty, 21/2/1922.
11 *Ibid.*, 10/3/1922.
12 *Ibid.*, 18/3/1922.
13 *Ibid.*, 14/3/1922.
14 Rex Taylor, *op. cit.*, p. 184.
15 Michael to Kitty, 28/3/1922 and 29/3/1922.
16 *Ibid.*, 30/3/1922.
17 Montgomery Hyde, *The Londonderrys*, p. 150.
18 Michael to Kitty, 31/3/1922.
19 Michael to Kitty, 10/4/1922 and Kitty to Michael, 10/4/1922.
20 Michael to Kitty, 14/4/1922.
21 *Ibid.*
22 *Ibid.*, 18/4/1922.
23 Cope to Churchill, 15/4/1922, telegram, 5.49 pm, CO 906/20.
24 Ernest Blythe to author, 20/3/1974; see Meda Ryan, *The Real*

Chief: the Story of Liam Lynch, pp. 107–110.
25 Ibid.
26 Michael Collins, The Path to Freedom, p. 17.
27 Ulick O'Connor, Oliver St John Gogarty, p. 188.
28 Kitty to Michael, 25/4/1922.
29 Michael to Kitty, 15/4/1922 and 18/4/1922.
30 Kitty to Michael, 16/2/1922.
31 Ibid., 26/4/1922.
32 Michael to Kitty, 27/4/1922.
33 Michael Collins to Hayden Talbot, q. Hayden Talbot, op. cit., p. 173.

'English Lady' under Suspicion

1 Reverend Frank Gibney, Passionist priest to a Cork nun, May 1922, q. Piaras Béaslaí, op cit., pp. V. II, 474.
2 Rex Taylor, op. cit., p. 184.
3 Michael to Kitty, 30/5/1922.
4 Ibid., 28/5/1922.
5 Terence de Vere White, p. 93.
6 Michael to Kitty, 31/5/1922.
7 Ibid.
8 Leon Ó Broin, In Great Haste, p. 181.
9 Ulick O'Connor, Sunday Independent, 15/9/1996.
10 Terence de Vere White, Kevin O'Higgins, p. 93.
11 Sir John Lavery, op. cit., p. 196.
12 Kitty to Michael, 15/7/1922.
13 Todd Andrews to author, 4/11/1983.
14 Sir John Lavery, op. cit., p. 197.
15 Emmet Dalton to Hazel Lavery, 15/11/1922, Lady Lavery Collection, q. McCoole, op. cit., p. 104.
16 Anonymous to Sir John Lavery, n. d. 1923, Lady Lavery Collection, q. McCoole, op. cit., p. 104.
17 Mícheál Ó Cuinneagáin, On the Arm of Time, p. 41 – for speculation. Correspondence from Richard Llewelyn-Davies, 10 Aug. 1974, 19 Sept. 1974 and telephone conversation, 26 Sept. 1974. Correspondence from Robert Barton, June 14 1974. Todd Andrews to author, 4/11/1983.

Women's Allegiance Split by Civil War

1 Tom Jones, *op. cit.*, pp. 206, 207.
2 PG Minutes, 12/6/1922, MP, P7/B/192; MP, 15/6/1922, UCDA.
3 Kitty to Michael, recd., 26/6/1922.
4 Michael to Kitty, 26/6/1922.
5 Meda Ryan, *The Day Michael Collins Was Shot*, pp. 17–21.
6 Lloyd George to Michael Collins 22/6/1922, MP, P7/B/244/1 and 2, UCDA.
7 Michael to Kitty, 28/6/1922.
8 PG Minutes, 30/6/1922, MP, P7/B/244/22.
9 Maud Gonne MacBride, *Éire: The Nation*, 28/9/1923.
10 Máire Comerford, unpublished memoirs.
11 Dorothy Macardle, *op. cit.*, 686.
12 Kitty to Michael, 7/7/1922.
13 Michael to Kitty, Government Buildings, 12/7/1922.
14 Michael to Kitty, 13/7/1922.
15 Kitty to Michael, c. 3/7/1922.
16 Michael to Kitty, 5/7/1922 and 12/7/1922.
17 PG Minutes, morning meeting 12/7/1922, MP, P7/B/244/58; also PRO. PG 57, 12/7/1922; 23. PG Minutes, evening meeting, 12/7/1922, MP, P7/B/244/61. See Meda Ryan, *op. cit.*, pp. 22–29.
18 Michael to Kitty, 12/7/1922.
19 *Ibid.*, 13/7/1922.
20 Kitty to Michael, 15/7/1922.
21 Meda Ryan, *The Day Michael Collins was Shot*, *op. cit.*, p. 34.
22 Michael to Kitty, 26/7/1922.
23 Boland/McGarrity correspondence, McGarrity Papers, NLI.
24 *Ibid.*, 25/7/1922.
25 Collins to Harry Boland, q. Taylor, *op. cit.*, p. 194.
26 Anna Fitzsimons-Kelly, *Irish Press*, 1/8/1938.
27 Collins to Director of Intelligence, 3/7/1922, MP, P7/B/4/90.
28 Michael to Kitty, c. 2/8/1922.
29 Kitty to Michael, recd. 4/8/1922.
30 Michael to Kitty, 4/8/1922.
31 Kitty to Michael, 15/7/1922.
32 Michael to Kitty, 14/7/1922.

Commander-in-Chief's August Days

1 Dr Gerard Ahern to author, 10/8/1974; See Meda Ryan, *op. cit.*, pp. 26, 176, 177.
2 Dr Gerard Ahern to author, 10/8/1974.
3 John L. O'Sullivan to author, 30/7/1974.
4 O'Duffy to C of GS, n. d., MP, P7/B/68.
5 Michael to Kitty, 8/8/1922.
6 *Ibid.*, 9/8/1922.
7 Ernest Blythe to author, 19/1/1974.
8 Collins' notebook, 12/8/1922, MP, P7a/62.
9 Michael to Kitty, 11/8/1922.
10 Collins' notes in diary, 16/8/1922, MP, P7a/62.
11 Collins' notes, NLI.
12 D. V. Horgan to author, 23/5/1922.
13 Collins, 16/8/1922, MP, P7/B/28/97.
14 Forester, *op. cit.*, p. 331.
15 Sir John Lavery, *op. cit.*, p. 216.
16 Collins' personal notes, MP, P7a/62.
17 General O'Duffy, GOC, South Western Division to Collins C. in C., MP, P7/B/39/32 & 33.
18 Commander-in-Chief to Officer Commanding S. W. Command 17/8/1922, MP, P7/B/21/8.
19 Frank O'Connor, *op. cit.*, *p.* 210.
20 Emmet Dalton to Collins, 19/8/1922, MP, P7/B/70/63 & P7/B/70/65.
21 Commander-in-Chief to General Dalton, 19/8/1922, P7/B/20/2.
22 Collins' notes, n. d. MP, P7/B/28/1.
23 Countess of Fingal, *op. cit.*, p. 403.
24 Piaras Béaslaí, *op. cit.*, pp. V. II, 429.
25 Kitty to Michael, 17/8/1922.
26 Sir John Lavery, *op. cit.*, p. 216.
27 Lady Gregory in her journal, pp. 180, 181.
28 Countess of Fingal, *op. cit.*, p. 409.
29 George Bernard Shaw to Hazel Lavery, q. Lavery, *op. cit.*, p. 218.
30 Sir John Lavery, *op. cit.*, p. 216.
31 *Ibid.*
32 Frank O'Connor, *op. cit.*, p. 211.
33 Michael to Kitty, 8/8/1922.

34 Kitty to Michael, 15/8/1922.
35 *Ibid.*, 16/8/1922.

Deep Mourning for Lover and Leader
1 Sir John Lavery, *op. cit.*, pp. 216, 217; Countess of Fingall, *op. cit.*, pp. 408, 409.
2 Daily newspapers, also MP, P7a/64.
3 Emmet Dalton to author, 20/4/1974.

Postscript
1 Sir John Lavery, *op. cit.*, pp. 218, 219.
2 Terence de Vere White, *op. cit.*, p. 93. Sinéad McCoole in her life of Hazel Lavery quotes romantic fragments of letters from O'Higgins to Lady Lavery 'censored by Hazel herself' and spanning some years.
3 Lavery, *op. cit.*, pp. 225–251.

BIBLIOGRAPHY

PRIMARY SOURCES

Private Sources

Michael Collins' diary and details of Collins' career from Michael Collins, a nephew; also details of Nancy O'Brien's (his mother's) activities from him

Mr Liam Collins, background information

Mary Collins-Powell, *Memoirs* and Helena Collins, *Memoirs* (Michael Collins' sisters), from Mary Clare O'Malley and Mary Collins-Pierce.

Hales private papers from Maura Murphy and Eily Hales-MacCarthy

Leslie Price de Barra: private papers and memoirs

Máire Comerford: private papers and memoirs

Máire (Killeen) Mulloy: private letters of Susan Killeen

Dorothy (Dicker) Heffernan: private letters, records and memorabilia of Dilly Dicker

David Neligan: private papers and memoirs

Liam O'Donoghue: private papers including Nancy O'Brien letters

Peter Barry Collection of Michael Collins, Kitty Kiernan and Lady Lavery letters

Íosold Ó Deirg: Sligo prison diary of Michael Collins which he gave to Sinéad Mason

Moya Llewelyn Davies: private letters from Diarmuid Brennan

Interviews with contemporaries of Michael Collins as cited in the Acknowledgements and Notes

Archives

University College, Dublin, Archives: Richard Mulcahy Papers; Ernest Blythe Papers; Ernie O'Malley Papers: Desmond Fitzgerald Papers.

Trinity College, Dublin: Erskine Childers Papers and Diaries.

National Library of Ireland: Michael Collins Papers; Joseph McGarrity Papers; Art O'Brien Papers; Austin Stack Papers;

Kathleen Napoli MacKenna Papers; Florrie O'Donoghue
Papers; Mark Sturgis' Diary.
Military Archives, Dublin: Captured Correspondence and Docu-
ments; Intelligence Reports; General Staff Instructions;
Operations Reports; Newspaper cuttings; Military Reports;
Ernie O'Malley notebooks.
State Paper Office, Dublin: Minutes of Provisional Government;
Minutes of the Executive Council; Dáil Éireann Papers.
Public Records: British Library Board Newspaper Library,
London; Colonial Office Papers, Public Record Office,
London.

Newspapers and Periodicals
*Irish Times, Irish Independent, Freeman's Journal, Cork Examiner,
Irish Press, Sunday Express, Daily Sketch, Daily Mail, Sunday
Independent, Sunday Press, Capuchin Annual, Police Gazette-
Hue and Cry, Sinn Féin Journal.*

SECONDARY SOURCES
Andrews, C. S., *Dublin Made Me*, Mercier Press, 1979.
Arthur, Sir G., *General Sir George Maxwell*, John Murray,
1932.
Barry, Tom, *Guerrilla Days in Ireland*, Irish Press 1949, Mercier
Press, 1955, Anvil Books, 1982.
Béaslaí, Piaras, *How It Was Done – IRA Intelligence: Dublin's
Fighting Story, 1916–1921*, Talbot Press, 1926.
————, *Michael Collins and the Making of a New Ireland*, 2 vols.,
Phoenix Publishing, 1926.
Bell, J. Bowyer, *The Secret Army*, Poolbeg Press, 1989.
Bennett, Richard, *The Black and Tans*, New English Library,
1970.
Birkenhead, Earl of, F. E., *The Life of F. E. Smith: First Earl of
Birkenhead*, Eyre & Spottiswoode, 1959.
Bowman, John, *De Valera and the Ulster Question, 1917–1973*,
Oxford University Press, 1982.
Breen, Dan, *My Fight for Irish Freedom*, Anvil Books, 1964.
Brennan, Michael, *The War in Clare*, Irish Academic Press,
1980.
Brennan, Robert, *Allegiance*, Irish Press, 1950.

Callwell, C. E., *Field-Marshal Sir Henry Wilson: His Life and Diaries*, 2 vols., Cassell, 1927.

Cartland, Barbara, *We Danced All Night*, Anchor Press, 1971.

Caulfield, Max, *The Easter Rebellion*, Frederick Muller, 1964.

Churchill, Winston, *The Aftermath*, Butterworth, 1929.

Clarke, Kathleen, *Revolutionary Woman*, The O'Brien Press, 1991.

Collins, Michael, *The Path to Freedom*, Mercier Press, 1968.

Colum, Pádraig, *Arthur Griffith*, Dublin, 1959.

Coogan, Tim Pat, *Ireland Since the Rising*, Pall Mall, 1966.

————,*The IRA*, Fontana, 1980.

————, *Michael Collins*, Hutchinson, 1990.

Countess of Fingall, Elizabeth, *Seventy Years Young*, Pall Mall, 1937.

Coxhead, Elizabeth, *Lady Gregory*, Macmillan, 1961.

Cronin, Bean, *The McGarrity Papers*, Anvil Books, 1972.

Crozier, Brigadier General F. P., *Ireland Forever*, Cape 1932.

Curran, Joseph M., *The Birth of the Irish Free State, 1921–1923*, Atlanta University Press, 1988.

Curtis, Liz, *The Cause of Ireland*, Beyond the Pale Publications, 1994.

Dalton, Charles, *With the Dublin Brigades 1917–21*, Peter Davies, 1929.

De Burca, Pádraig and John F. Boyle, *Free State or Republic?*, Talbot Press and Fisher Unwin, 1922.

Deasy, Liam, *Towards Ireland Free*, Mercier Press, 1979.

De Vere White, Terence, *Kevin O'Higgins*, Methuen, 1948.

Dudley Edwards, Ruth, *Patrick Pearse, The Triumph of Failure*, Poolbeg Press, 1990.

Dwyer, T. Ryle, *Michael Collins and the Treaty*, Mercier Press, 1981.

————, *De Valera's Darkest Hour, 1919–32*, Mercier Press, 1982.

————, *Michael Collins – The Man Who Won the War*, Mercier Press, 1990.

————, *De Valera – The Man and the Myth*, Poolbeg Press, 1990.

Fallon, Charlotte H., *Soul of Fire*, Mercier Press, 1986.

Fanning, Ronan, *Independent Ireland*, Helicon, 1983.

Farrell, Michael, *Northern Ireland, The Orange State*, London, 1975.

————, *Arming Protestants*, Brandon Book Publishing and Pluto Press, 1983.

Figgis, Darrell, *Recollections of the Irish War*, London, 1927.

Fitzpatrick, David, *Politics and Irish Life 1913–21*, Gill and Macmillan, 1977.

Forester, Margery, *Michael Collins: The Lost Leader*, Sidgwick and Jackson, 1971.

Foster, Roy, *Modern Ireland, 1600–1972*, Allen Lane, 1988.

Garvin, Tom, *The Evolution of Irish Nationalist Politics*, Gill and Macmillan, 1981.

Gaughan, J. A., Austin Stack, *Portrait of a Separatist*, Kingdom, 1977.

Mee, Jeremiah, *The Memoirs of Constable Jeremiah Mee*, R. I. C., Dublin, 1975.

Geary, Laurence, *Plan of Campaign*, Cork University Press, 1986.

Gleeson, James, *Bloody Sunday*, London, 1962.

Gogarty, Oliver St John, *As I Was Going Down Sackville Street*, Richard Cowen, 1937.

Greaves, C. D., *Liam Mellows and the Irish Revolution*, Lawrence & Wishart, 1971.

Griffith, Kenneth and Timothy E. O'Grady, *Curious Journey*, 1982.

Healy, J. M., *Letters and Leaders of My Day*, Vol. II, Thornton Butterworth, 1928.

Hopkinson, Michael, *Green Against Green*, Gill and Macmillan, 1988.

Hyde, Montgomery, *The Londonderrys*, Hamish Hamilton, 1979.

Jones, Tom, *Whitehall Diaries*, Vol. III, Oxford University Press, 1970.

Kee, Robert, *Ourselves Alone; The Green Flag*, Vol. 3, Quartet Books, 1976.

Kerryman, ed. *Dublin's Fighting Story, 1916–1921; Rebel Cork's Fighting Story; Sworn to be Free: the Complete Book of IRA Jailbreaks, 1918–1921*, Kerryman, 1971.

Laffan, Michael, *The Partition of Ireland*, Dundalgan Press, Dundalk, 1983.

Lavery, Sir John, *The Life of a Painter*, Cassell, 1940.

Lawlor, Sheila, *Britain and Ireland, 1914–23*, Gill and Macmillan, 1981.

Lee, J. J., and Ó Tuathaigh, Gearóid, *The Age of de Valera*, Ward River Press and RTÉ, 1982.

Lee, J. J., *Ireland 1912–1985*, Cambridge University Press, 1989.

Longford, Earl of and Thomas P. O'Neill, *Eamon De Valera*, London and Dublin, 1970.

Lyons, F. S. L., *Ireland Since the Famine*, Collins/Fontana, 1973.

Lyons, J. B., *Oliver St John Gogarty*, Blackwater Press, 1980.

Macardle, Dorothy, *The Irish Republic*, Corgi, 1968.

MacEoin, Uinseann, ed., *Survivors*, Argenta, 1980.

Macready, Sir Nevil, *Annals of an Active Life*, Hutchinson, 1942.

Mackay, James, *Michael Collins: A Life*, Mainstream Publishing, 1996.

McCoole, Sinéad, *Hazel – A Life of Lady Lavery*, The Lilliput Press, 1996.

Martin, F. X., ed., *The Irish Volunteers 1913–15*, James Duffy, 1963.

Martin, F. X., ed., *Leaders and Men of the Easter Rising*, Methuen, 1965.

Morrison, George, *The Irish Civil War: An Illustrated History*, Dublin, Gill and Macmillan, 1991.

Murphy, Brian P., *Patrick Pearse and the Lost Republican Ideal*, James Duffy, 1981.

Murphy, John A., *Ireland in the Twentieth Century*, Gill and Macmillan, 1975.

Neeson, Eoin, *The Life and Death of Michael Collins*, Mercier Press, 1968

———, *The Civil War 1922–1923*, Poolbeg Press, 1989.

Neligan, David, *The Spy in the Castle*, MacGibbon & Kee, 1968.

Ní Dheirg, Íosold, *The Story of Michael Collins*, Mercier Press, 1978.

O'Broin, Leon, *Michael Collins*, Gill and Macmillan, 1980

———, *Revolutionary Underground – The Story of the IRB, 1825–1924*, Gill and Macmillan, 1983.

———, (ed.), *In Great Haste, the Letters of Michael Collins and Kitty Kiernan*, (revised, Cian Ó hEigeartaigh (ed.), 1996.

O'Connor, Batt, *With Michael Collins in the Fight for Irish Independence*, Peter Davies, 1929.

O'Connor, Frank, *The Big Fellow*, Poolbeg Press, 1979.

O'Connor, Ulick, *A Terrible Beauty is Born*, Hamish Hamilton, 1975.

———, *Oliver St John Gogarty*, Granada, 1981.

O'Donoghue, Florence, *No Other Law*, Irish Press, 1954.

———, *Tomás MacCurtain*, Anvil, 1971.

O'Farrell, Patrick, *Ireland's English Question*, Schocken, 1971.

O'Halloran, Clare, *Partition and the Limits of Ideology*, Gill and Macmillan, 1989.

O'Hegarty, P. S., *The Victory of Sinn Féin*, Talbot Press, 1924.

O'Mahony, Seán, *Frongoch: University of Revolution*, Dublin 1987.

O'Malley, Ernie, *On Another Man's Wound*, Anvil Books, 1972.

———, *The Singing Flame*, Anvil Books, 1979.

O'Neill, Máire, *A Biography of Jennie Wyse-Power*, Blackwater Press, 1991.

Pakenham, Frank, *Peace by Ordeal*, Sidgwick & Jackson, 1972.

Roskill, S. W., *Hankey, Man of Secrets*, Vol. II, Collins, 1972.

Ryan, Desmond, *Remembering Sion*, Baker, 1936.

———, *Michael Collins and the Invisible Army*, Anvil Books, 1932.

Ryan, Meda, *The Day Michael Collins Was Shot*, Poolbeg Press, 1989.

———, *The Real Chief – The Story of Liam Lynch*, Mercier Press, 1986.

———, *The Tom Barry Story*, Mercier Press, 1982.

Salvidge, Stanley, *Salvidge of Liverpool*, London, 1934.

Scott, C. P., ed., T. Wilson, *Political Diaries, 1911–28*, Collins, 1970.

Shakespear, Sir Geoffrey, *Let Candles be Brought In*, MacDonald, 1949.

Talbot, Hayden, *Michael Collins' Own Story*, Hutchinson, 1923.

Taylor, Rex, *Michael Collins*, Four Square, 1961

———, *Assassination: The Death of Sir Henry Wilson*, Hutchinson, 1961.

Townsend, Charles, *The British Campaign in Ireland, 1919–21*, Oxford University Press, 1975.

Ward, Margaret, *Unmanageable Revolutionaries*, Brandon, 1983.

Winter, Ormonde, *Winter's Tale*, Richards Press, 1955.
Younger, Calton, *Ireland's Civil War*, Frederick Muller, 1972

INDEX